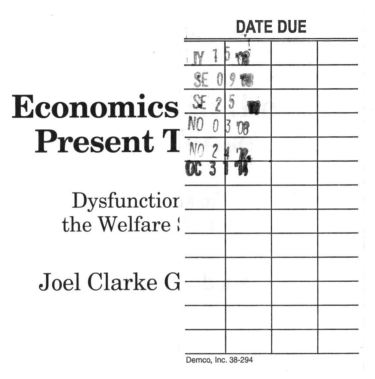

DATE DUE

JY 1 5 '8			
SE 0 9 '8			
SE 2 5 '8			
NO 0 3 08			
NO 2 4 '8			
OC 3 1 '8			

Demco, Inc. 38-294

Economics

Present T

Dysfunctior
the Welfare !

Joel Clarke G

VANTAGE PRESS
New York

Cover design by Polly McQuillen

FIRST EDITION

Published by Vantage Press, Inc.
419 Park Ave. South, New York, NY 10016

Manufactured in the United States of America
ISBN: 978-0-533-15740-2

Library of Congress Catalog Card No.: 2007900867

0 9 8 7 6 5 4 3 2 1

For my father, Frank Gibbons, and for Crispina, Marcus,
Eileen, and Hugh, and all those who love them

Contents

**Two Essays on the Financial and
Commodity Markets**

Introduction

The wealth of any nation is equal to the productivity of her people. There is no other measure of national prosperity that stands scrutiny. Other measures are more or less consistent with this one, and for that reason can not be dismissed, but they are only indirect and derivative standards of wealth.

Nation states are very enthusiastic about gaining wealth and power in the community of nations. They count influence amongst their neighbors as a good and as an end in itself. One of the fruits of such power is wealth. The prophet of the Old Testament, writing eloquently of the age when the Messiah reigns, promised that the wealth of nations would be spread before his throne in Israel; that camels from the four corners of the Earth would toil unceasingly just to deliver the largess of the world to Jerusalem. It is indeed a pleasant reverie, but if these words are taken literally, they are not a promise of wealth. They are a promise of leisure, but leisure is not wealth. My father, the only child of an abandoned mother who came to this country to work as a maid in the homes of wealthy Bostonians, had his first job delivering groceries from a horse-drawn wagon. He was nine years of age. He continued to work while he finished his studies, and when he reached the normal retirement age he had served as a vice president and director of a major S&P 500 corporation and as the president of his country club. From the poverty of south Boston to the leafy north shore suburbs of Chicago, he had worked for well over a half century. In retirement he continued to volunteer his time and talents well into his 90's. He had one simple bit of advice for us: "Don't complain when someone tells you to work. Complain when they tell you *not* to work."

Leisure is a wonderful thing. It is good in itself and it is an integral part of every other aspect of our lives. Without it, and without being able to enjoy it, we go mad and lose our way. Not only do we enjoy leisure, we look forward eagerly to the kind of sumptuous lifestyle promised by the prophet. It is quite understandable therefore that governments are eager to apply whatever power and influence they can garner to guarantee their share—or more than their share—of the wealth of nations and to fill the in-bound lanes of their highways with heavy-laden camels. In doing so they expect to earn amongst other things the gratitude and loyalty of their citizens.

The Old Testament vision of the wealth of nations famously inspired Adam Smith and became the title of his most influential treatise. But while the title was ancient, the promise he made was at least superficially very different. Isaiah was short on details. All that he saw clearly was the simple cause and effect: first the Messiah arrives, then and as a direct result, the camels follow shortly. Adam Smith by contrast saw the details. What he saw was, to summarize, that if the sovereign would leave his subjects to employ their ambitions and skills for their own well-being, the promise of Isaiah would be achieved. Superficially what makes this a departure is that it doesn't seem to depend on a Messiah, but that is misleading. Isaiah never predicted that the Messiah would force prosperity on lazy and indifferent subjects; he only promised that because there is a Messiah, virtue and hard work will be rewarded. He was not interested in the details, and chose to leave them to the Messiah.

The substantive difference, the great innovation of Adam Smith, was to see that the homely cause and effect from honesty, ambition, and hard work to prosperity is more than just a bit of good advice that parents share with their children. It is universal and natural law that regulates—not excluding other equally fundamental laws, but together with them—the business affairs of the world and the wealth of nations. Thus we acknowledge the causal bridge that runs from personal virtues to wealth, and in so doing we recognize the truth that the wealth of a nation is the productivity of her people: not how well they live or how much they consume, but how wisely they live and how much they create.

That is the topic of this small book, which is the sequel to my earlier work, *Rethinking the Headlines*. The two books are however very different in their subject matter. *Rethinking the Headlines* is a book of political theory, and more particularly of the legal framework of law and government, applied to some of the hottest political issues in America today. My goal for this book is to take some of the best insights of economic science, which are by nature timeless principles, and apply them concretely to America today. We are bombarded with news about economic and business affairs. It is possible, or to be more exact it is very easy, to stay current on the stock market on a minute-by-minute basis. Every day the headlines scream out some factoid of presumed importance, whether the trade gap or the latest claims for unemployment insurance. Behind the wave of headlines comes a second wave of "interpretation." I enclose that word in quotation marks for obvious reasons: I find very little interpretation and lots of hype in those columns. They keep coming anyway, because they serve someone's interests.

Most telling however, where one awaits a third wave of deeper thought, it never seems to arrive. Tomorrow brings new factoids and the day after tomorrow follows up with new interpretation. There is seemingly no room left in our papers for a second thought. There is much good thinking and good writing about economic affairs, because Americans are quite economically literate. Many insightful newsletters and professional commentators. Some excellent books and longer articles also. I have no conscious agenda of where or how I can add to this information. It might be that I have nothing to add, and at best regurgitate well-known truths. Presumably in that case lagging book sales will deliver the embarrassing message. Whatever I do have to add, in any case, will have to emerge from the agenda stated above: to see current events in the light of enduring economic theory.

The casual reader will almost surely see in this book a very different common thread, which is that in America today things are not as good as they seem. Mine is by no means the first book in recent times to make that statement nor, surely, will it be the last. The public is aware, in a visceral way, that some important things are going wrong. The public media have tried very hard for many years to paint the rosiest picture they could. Glowing speculation is frequently reported as fact. Unpleasant headlines are immediately doused with reams of explanation. No effort is spared to convey a *Positive Message,* rather than to delve into the ambiguities and the sometimes unpleasant side of current events. It turns out however that Abraham Lincoln was right: it is possible to fool all the people some of the time and to fool some of the people all of the time, but it is impossible to fool all the people all the time. If the people want to make changes, they will make changes, but they first have to understand what is going on.

My credentials in this way may not seem impressive. I am not privy to any state secrets or to the services of any board of certified experts. I have to rely on my own education and experience. I have had immense and no doubt undeserved good fortune in my education. I took honors in physics at Georgetown University. After a year in law school at the University of Chicago, I transferred to the department of mathematics at Northwestern University. Like many of those who graduated with their doctoral degrees in 1970, I graduated without a job. After a couple of years spent proving that my predicament was indeed as serious as it seemed, I matriculated at the Graduate School of Business of the University of Chicago. It was there that I fell in love with the science of economics, and it was there that I took first an M.B.A. and then a doctorate in economics. My natural inclinations drew me into business rather than into academia, and the scintillating lure of the commodity markets in Chicago proved too compelling to resist. After a dozen years spent working for two very large banks in Chicago, I opened my own independent commodity trading company and began to work without a net, wagering my own little capital and my clients' money every day.

The Internet is the source of most of my news and data, although there is no need to apologize for what is available on the Internet. It is a miracle of knowledge, equal in importance to the discovery of printing and to the telephone. Years of work in the financial industry, as a trader and strategist, have trained my powers of perception just as they have nourished my scepticism. In any case, I console myself with the realization that the wise reader will not stop with this book or with any single book, but will read broadly and will track down the key data that will enable him to draw his own conclusions, and he will have to apply his own judgment and intuition along the way.

The question to which he will apply them is however very clear. We as a nation have let our talents waste and our skills rust. We have not devoted ourselves as we need to the task of enhancing our productivity. We have become complacent in our manifest wealth, and have not added to it in recent years but have eaten into it. We live well by consuming more than we produce, and for a long time our magnificent standard of living has obscured the truth.

This book is divided into three general sections. The first one takes up various timely issues, but makes the single point about our productivity. The second section is devoted to analyzing one particular ramification of this broader story: the inflation risk that hangs over our economy and our financial markets at this time. The third section is a collection of essays on topics in economics which applies economic thought to specific topics of contemporary interest. Many of these essays are bits of lectures and readings that I created for various courses in economics and finance. It has been my good fortune to have taught for eight years in the Stuart School of Business at Illinois Institute of Technology, and to have taught more briefly at many other colleges and universities. Over the years I have taught in community colleges and in a state university that is in effect an inner city public school, and on the other hand I have taught at the University of Chicago, and have lectured extensively at that university and others of considerable renown. One of my most cherished accomplishments is to have lectured in four different divisions of the University of Chicago.[1] Throughout this book I will have some rather pointed—I am reluctant to say "harsh," but the reader can judge for himself—observations about the state of education in America. Indeed, no issue is more central to this book than the state of education, and so my remarks are not merely diversions. As I indulge in commenting on the present state of education, at least it must be granted that I speak and write from direct experience.

The topic of education is so vitally important today however that the reader should not be content with my comments, but should use the very large body of reports and analysis on the topic that is available today. The need for redirection of the whole educational industry, from kindergarten to graduate school, is much too important and too pressing for anyone to settle comfortably for anything less than the best available information. Since however this is not a book about education as such, I absolve myself from laying out the necessary data, but the American public, whose education is at stake, needs to know more. Get informed, and then demand reform.

The ideas expressed in these pages owe much to many great thinkers, and especially to the faculty of the University of Chicago whose contributions to economic science have transformed it utterly. One of them—a man whose career stretched from Vienna to Chicago and back—is Frederick von Hayek. His seminal work entitled *The Road to Serfdom* has become forgotten by a world that thinks that the public dole is a bargain but human rights and freedoms are too expensive. From his uniquely Austrian perspective, writing in the aftermath of the Second World War, he saw too clearly how bad a bargain that is.

The American people have always been optimistic

and industrious. It is not by their choice that their optimism has been exploited and their industriousness wasted. We need to rebuild America, to believe as we always did that our wealth is measured by the productivity of the people. We need to get back to work. Economics is about everyday reality, so it always exists in the present tense. It is my fond hope that this little book will contribute to that awakening to economics in the present tense.

Joel C. Gibbons
Saint Joseph, Michigan
November, 2006

Notes

1. The Department of Mathematics, the Graduate School of Business, the School Service Administration, and what is now the Harris School of Public Policy, which was in those days the Committee on Public Policy Studies.

Economics in the
Present Tense

1
On Work

Every measure of national income or product—e.g. Gross Domestic Product—is a measure of Effort Expended. There is no known national measure of Results Obtained.

The wealth of a nation is defined by and is measured in terms of the work that is done there.[1] Work, in this context, is similar to labor but they are by no means the same thing. Perhaps we should start by clarifying the difference between work and labor. Labor is expended but work is accomplished. We labor because we must and we work because we can. Labor is for a proximate reward, usually a pay check. Labor is defined by the need for that reward, and there is absolutely nothing mean or contemptible about that. Even those who are now retired once labored, and were blessed to make a living that supported us and our families. Labor is good because the results are good, but it is not defined by the product thereof. The product of our labor is some thing: trees pruned and lawns mowed, sonatas performed or lines of poetry penned, diapers changed or rooms dusted. Labor is however measured by effort, rather than by results, and by the rewards that effort earns. Work by contrast is defined by the results achieved. When we work toward some accomplishment we are working. The difference is unmistakably clear in practice: we naturally love work but we resent labor.

1

This sums up the psychology of work, so to speak, but that is only one side of it. We can not define work until we fix some measure of accomplishment. We call that measure *value*. When it is a product that is bought and sold in exchange for other goods it is natural to put value on a money scale. Money measures how much benefit our work provides to those whom it is intended to serve. As Peter Drucker emphasized repeatedly, all results in the business sphere have to be judged by a market test: how much do the beneficiaries want it, and how much are they willing to pay for it. That principle extends beyond business as such, to the concept of work in every sphere.

It seems at first blush that there are many kinds of work that cannot be fitted to a scale of economic value. Charitable work is often assumed to be its own reward, because there is no equal exchange of value. Helping the poor and singing in the choir are commonly thought to be non-economic pursuits, but that is a misconception. The satisfaction one derives from feeding the needy is a subjective good, a reward that exists only in the mind of the charitable worker, but there is nothing subjective about the value of work. Its value is measured in terms not of the worker, but in terms of the beneficiary. If the needy are being nourished, that charity is valuable, but if somehow the charity is misguided and no one is actually benefiting, no work is being done because no value is being created. The subjective value which a charitable worker receives may be a substitute in his mind for money, and as a result he may be willing to donate his labor. There is however a world of differences between unpaid work and ineffective, valueless toil. The former is work that is given for free because the beneficiary cannot pay its value in cash. The other, to repeat, is not work at all. Every effort that actually benefits someone, that creates value, is economic effort.

Work that families do for their members and labor that one member donates for the benefit of others are often work of a very high order, even if they are unpaid. This is the best and the most quantitatively significant example of unpaid work. The domestic economy knows how to value the work of its members and how to reward them, in ways that do not show up as anyone's taxable income.

One universal aspect of work is that it is learned. More than that, it is continuously perfected by training, experience, and sometimes formal education. It is always necessary to improve our work, and it is always possible. Any task can be polished to some extent, and usually to a great extent. Stuffing envelopes with advertising flyers demands no particular training, but anyone who does that job for a while gets faster and more reliable. Playing scales on the piano is the same. Playing music on the piano is a very high order of skill and education, but playing scales is not very different from stuffing envelopes. Yet this skill is the cornerstone of the piano; it must be mastered before the student can even contemplate playing classical sonatas. Each worker or student thinks of himself or herself as improving in one way or another and does not generalize to the country as a whole, but the economy generalizes for him.

The wealth of the nation results from the lifting of all these skills and the gaining of valuable knowledge one citizen and one task at a time. While every task admits of improvement however, higher skills are more precious than simple ones. "Higher order" simply means jobs and skills which have the largest gap in performance between the top workers and the slowest ones. Composing poetry is a high order task because of the gap between the poet whose lines are genuine and lasting, on the one hand, and the neophyte who as yet has little of worth to say and even less mastery of the tools to accomplish it. Every poet started with little more than a pencil and paper and burning desire. Some progressed, and some of those achieved immortality. If poetry were of small worth, this would not be a very interesting example, but amongst writers the poet has a unique place. We learn most of what we know from prose, obviously, but we only remember poetry. It is the only literature where we remember not only what is written, but also the way it is expressed, because in poetry form and content are inseparable.[2]

The success of a community and of an economy is for the most part measured by the work that is done there. The public are accordingly hopeful that their public authorities will look for ways to promote it, as promoting the general welfare. This has however proved to be an elusive goal. We attribute to Adam Smith the proposition that policies and programs of the government are highly unlikely to improve the general welfare, and that it would be better if they didn't try. His reasoning is very simple, really. Prosperity arises from applying every valuable tool and skill to its most valued purpose, and that is precisely what the owner would do without needing to be told. The government could not possibly have either a more intense desire or a more powerful motivation than the owner does. If the government wants to put the tools and skills of the community to some end different from what the owners would want, it must be that the public authorities do not want to use these economic assets in the most productive way. That is the *laissez-faire* doctrine according to Adam Smith.

This reasoning is too simple; it makes assumptions

that are frequently invalid. But as a practical matter it resonates. The example of numerous socialist countries serves to demonstrate that public decisions are in reality far more likely to destroy value and to waste work than they are to create value and promote work. The central limitation of the simple *laissez-faire* doctrine of Adam Smith is that the standard of highest value is not an invariant fact. Roads provide a good example. One of the things that governments do is to build roads, and they usually do so in a very socialistic way, meaning that they do not charge for the use of the road, but let anyone use it for free. A well-planned road justifies itself by enhancing the lives and the value of the work product of those citizens that use it. If they make something, they can now sell it over a broader market. If they provide services to others, they can now reach further to find persons who attach a high value to what they do. Value is not an absolute that is defined and fixed in the individual—whether that means an individual asset, or a single person, or a single idea—but it is the joint result of countless intersecting works that sometimes compete with it as alternatives and that otherwise complement it as parts of a more distant whole. That is why the science of economics is not a branch of engineering but is a social science. Thus, Adam Smith notwithstanding, the public authorities have a contribution to make in enhancing the prosperity of the community.[3] Adam Smith dealt in broad principles, but any assessment of the effectiveness of government and "rules" depends on a weighing of actual costs and benefits—in the same way that we appraise any other activity—and cannot be decided on general principles.

A strange and dangerous fallacy has however inserted itself into the way we look at the role of the government in economic affairs, growing out of a confusion of work and labor, and it is a fallacy that Adam Smith would have recognized instantly. It is taken as a given that the national government should put people to labor. This is more often expressed clumsily as a policy to "create jobs." While all labor is noble for the laborer, not all labor is good. Few tasks, for instance, were more laborious than breaking rock on the chain gang but there is little call to bring back the chain gang or to assign ordinary citizens to it. Expressed somewhat differently, the one community that has definitely solved the jobs problem is a slave labor camp. I will argue in these pages that in America today, we have a problem caused by too many jobs but too little work. Our public commitment to jobs does serve to feed the flock, to spread sustenance to everyone who is physically and mentally capable to hold a job. What it does not do is to create value, or to help the public to create value of their own. In practice it seems to have encouraged many to waste their time on make-work tasks which only distract us from real work.

I will argue in these pages that in America today, we have a problem caused by too many jobs, but too little work. We keep nearly everyone busy, because we can do that.

Capital: Technology and Tools

Since this chapter is devoted to setting out some important concepts that deal with labor and work, it is the best place to take a comparable look at capital. Capital is simply money spent—that is to say, value expended—to produce something or some skill or knowledge that is valued not for itself, but for how it contributes to the value of work. Before one sets off to drive for the first time to a distant place, he spends some time poring over the map in order to avoid wasting far more time and aggravation when he is lost along the way. The time spent on the map is capital, or more properly it is the value of that time that is the capital, because capital is always measured in terms of value, and the decision to spend that time is investment. One invariable dimension of capital is Investment Risk, which is simply our term to describe the fact that when the investment is done there is no way of knowing the value it will actually provide. The map is most valuable when the route is obscure and hard to follow. If the route is well marked and simple, all that poring over the map will have been unnecessary effort and its value lost, but when the driver first opens his maps there is no way to know which it is.

The characteristic mark of modern economies is the amount of investment that every worker wields. Land is a kind of capital even though it is not produced, because it makes agriculture and animal husbandry possible. A millennium ago, land constituted nearly the whole body of capital, but today it is only a fraction. The rest consists of things like systematic knowledge, which is produced by the accretion of scholarly research, and all sorts of intelligent tools, especially the computer. The tools revolution started with large scale manufacturing of steel. All manner of saws, drills, hammers, and other hand tools followed. The roots of the industrial revolution can be traced back to Renaissance times, beginning with systematic research in agriculture, chemistry, and metallurgy.

Initially, capital served labor by enhancing the productivity of anyone who mastered its use. Apprentice programs of all sorts, including medicine and law, transmitted the relevant body of knowledge, and practice with the tools of the trade produced mastery in using them. It was not until the advent of the so-called "industrial revolution" the capital and labor became adversaries. The revolution consisted of a new kind of tool, machines of immense size and productivity. The simple hammer served the tinker well, but his descendants were forced to serve the gigantic hammer mill. Economies of scale reduced the worker to a servant just as engineering developments took much of what had been personal crafts and embedded them in the machine. The power of this new capital separated the few who were rich enough to own one of the precious machines of modern industry from their serfs who toiled to keep the machines fed.

Karl Marx, a remarkably astute observer of industry and of how technology was leaving its imprint on society, witnessed the degradation of work, but he could not anticipate how the explosive spread of knowledge—knowledge capital—would return to the worker the command of his tools. In no other respect in this truer than the personal computer and the Internet. The knowledge revolution that began perhaps five hundred years ago is now resolved, as the tools—both mechanical and knowledge—of the craftsman and craftswoman have been returned to them, but transformed from dumb steel and fiber to computer-guided terminals and Internet, which gives access to all the world's recorded knowledge. The access to knowledge is even more remarkable than the growth of knowledge *per se,* but it is restricted to those able to use it.

The computer revolution has another side that is as important as the Internet. Industry has harvested a century of research in physics, chemistry, and biology to produce instruments that nearly run themselves, and the development of the silicon chip has made it possible to embed a high level of artificial intelligence in them. One class of intelligence is the ability to initiate an appropriate and timely response to prevailing conditions as they emerge. Technology now endows all sorts of objects with sensors to observe the environment and to feed that information to a microprocessor programmed to respond. While this intelligence is in every way "artificial," because it consists merely of repeating instructions that were imprinted in memory when it was made, the resulting instrument has advantages of consistency that even we mortals can not match. There are many tasks that are done better by a microprocessor than by one of us. It is possible moreover to link intelligent instruments together into entire factories that operate nearly without any human intervention. The Allen-Bradley Company of Milwaukee, now a subsidiary of Rockwell International, introduced a factory twenty years ago that accepted orders electronically from its customers, filled the orders on an assembly line, packaged the completed order, and placed it on the shipping dock. The only human intervention needed was maintenance—because the machines lacked the capacity to repair themselves or to correct accidents in the process—and resupply with the parts used in the assembly phase.[4]

This factory makes about one hundred different products from the Allen-Bradley catalog. A century ago, when machines were massively powerful but deaf and dumb, economies of scale dictated huge production runs of a few product varieties. The automated, intelligent factory is not constrained by economies of scale. If the next order that a customer places calls for one each of all the hundred models, the assembly line will fill that order as easily as if it called for one hundred identical pieces. There are many areas of the economy where scale economies dominate, and many of them appear at this time to be inevitable, but the combination of automated intelligence and the capacity to respond to instructions and to environmental conditions have vastly reduced the scope of economies of scale.

The knowledge revolution has no native language; it is at home and ready to serve in every human tongue. Whether it is the knowledge base that supports and informs the physician's judgment or the computer-controlled robot that burns semiconductor wafers, it serves the hands that guide it without regard to race, creed, or nationality.

In Conclusion

The future belongs to those who work with the knowledge revolution. No nation will own it, or deprive anyone else of the use of it. The capital of modern economics is not land, though land is still important, nor is it embodied in the giant dumb machines of the nineteenth century. Those machines also have not gone away, but capital today is myriad of tools and depths of knowledge that serve the worker rather than imprisoning him.

Notes

1. This proposition is not the same as the Marxian Labor Theory of Value. Investment is as much a contributor to what is produced in a given year as is the work done that year, and has as legitimate a claim to its share of the product. But investment in tools and ideas do not create themselves. There is moreover a special sort of work that foresees and manages the job, which Marxians assigned to capital, but is a very high order of work. These ideas are generally associated with the so-called Austrian School of Economics and with Joseph Schumpeter and Frederick Hayek. They trace back also to the founder of the University of Chicago school of economic theory, Frank Knight. See. Frank Knight. Risk,

Uncertainty, and Profit. Reprinted by Dover Publications, 2006. Marx was however by no means contemptuous of capital. His enemy was not the machines—which he admired—but the power that ownership of the machines gave to an abusive few.

2. This fact is easily verified. I don't know of any person could recite verbatim from the body of the Constitution or from the works of Einstein, but nearly everyone can recite children's rhymes.

3. I do not mean to suggest that the sole contribution of the government to the welfare of the community is exclusively, or even primarily, economic. Citizens surrender some of their freedom to their government and make common cause with their neighbors for other, equally important reasons also.

4. More timely and exhaustive information are available at their web site: www.rockwellautomation.com.

2

Cheap Labor

Recent trends in the labor market tell a disturbing story of American labor productivity, and it is to that story that we now turn. To summarize the labor market story, we have witnessed more people going to work—including in particular a suspiciously large number of illegal aliens—for ever lower wages. I will begin by surveying the evidence on this point, and following that I will try to sort out what it signifies in economic terms.

The American Dream: More Work for Lower Pay

From an economist's perspective, the single most important characteristic of labor is that it is not a homogenous commodity—just so many days of work—but is by contrast a cooperative endeavor of many different kinds of labor. Bosses need laborers to boss around, and laborers need bosses to create the work environment where they can be productive. Industrialists need accountants to keep track of how well they are or are not doing, and accountants need industrialists to produce the products and the sales and costs that are being accounted for. Sopranos need pianists to accompany them. Pianists are perhaps not so sure they need anyone else, but even they do. The demand for "labor" is therefore a series of uses for different kinds of laborers, and it depends on what laborers and what capital facilities are already in place, and how these pieces fit together.

The capacity that a single worker has to use the available tools and cooperating labor is called "human capital." It is the expandability of human effort, a measure of how much work the person can do. The systematic study of human capital formation began about forty years ago, led by Professor Gary Becker.[1] Human capital is not fungible. It is specific to the person and builds on endowments of birth and accidents of life which give some people potential as sopranos while others have their future as pianists. It is moreover elicited by opportunity defined by the economy, the society, and the technology that are each person's immediate environment. Because of the complexity of the environment, each person has actually many different potentials—many different points at which he can connect to the environment—and thus many alternative ways in which to be a success. It is sufficient to take advantage of any one of them. The term human capital was chosen to emphasize the investment of time and effort by which the person grows and develops his or her opportunities. Whatever those opportunities may be, it is by effort and patience that the person turns potential into capacity.

A recent report on consumer finances, produced by the staff of the Federal Reserve Board,[2] asserts that in real terms wage and salary income of Americans fell 6% between 2001 and 2004. Two processes are at work, combining to produce this startling finding. One thing that did not happen was for the average pay to fall for any specific occupation. Everyone who kept his or her job saw his pay rise. On the other hand, the purchasing power of those wages did not necessarily rise because the cost of living also rose at a pretty high rate. So, in summary, one process was inflation catching up to wages and salaries. The other process was change in the composition of the work, with higher paid workers losing their jobs—or retiring and not being replaced—while low paying jobs were hiring. The "average" wage and salary income in the Fed report is simply the average of all those people with jobs, at two different points in time, and it reflects not only what has happened to the people who were working at both times, but also the turnover in the labor force and the turnover of the jobs they do. However we parse the decline in wages—however we carve up the numbers—we arrive at the same conclusion, which is that there is a lack of investment in human capital.

Human capital expands the effective work of an individual. It is evident that a very large portion of the American population is not acquiring human capital. This is not due to laziness or indifference. Americans spend far more years in school than ever before, and more than any other people. They buy computers and dedicate themselves to learning to use them. They send their children to private tutors when the elementary and secondary schools fail them. Americans are ambitious and optimistic people. Yet on the whole they are not accumulating human capital as their parents and grandparents did. In part we can and must lay some of the blame on the educational system, but there is more to the story. So many of the industries that demand and reward human capital are the ones we are losing, and so many of the industries that are growing offer comparatively little opportunity for the worker to broaden and deepen his skills. That is the difference, of course, between a job that gives the worker freedom to innovate, and a job—like greeting customers at WalMart—that does not. The difference between the best and the ordinary biologist is enormous, perhaps orders of magnitude, while the difference between the best and the ordinary greeter is almost imperceptible. The work that every nation and every community needs to promote is the work with the biggest difference between ordinary and superb.

There is no lack of data on employment and pay, courtesy of the Bureau of Labor Statistics. The detail it shows is illuminating, but for our immediate purposes the simpler labor data collected by the Federal Reserve Board which covers more than a half century of history serves just as well. I have summarized this history in the following graph, which shows the trend of manufacturing and private sector service employment since 1952. It comes as quite a surprise that total manufacturing employment is lower today than it was in 1952. To some extent it should not be surprising, because in 1952 the factory workshop of Europe was still crippled by the world war, and Japan had hardly begun to build its industrial strength. America was by default the factory of the world at that time. It was inevitable that as Europe and Japan got back to work, their manufacturers would replace ours to some extent. The shrinking manufacturing headcount also has to some extent been offset by rising labor productivity, which is the byproduct of technological innovations in factory tools and controls, but rising productivity accounts for only a small part of the difference. America's factories today are world class, but there are many fewer of them than there were in 1952. The lion's share of the story has to be ascribed to abandonment of manufacturing industry in America and to rising imports of manufactured goods.

15

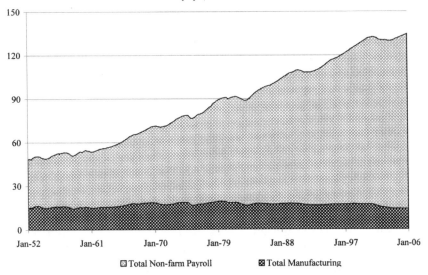

Civilian Employment History:
employment in millions

☐ Total Non-farm Payroll ☒ Total Manufacturing

Source: Federal Reserve Board and Logistic Research & Trading Co.

Why would we withdraw from manufacturing, and what are the consequences of that decision? We have not given up on manufacturing because we have other opportunities that pay better. The fact that wages have fallen in real terms demonstrates that we have replaced high paying industrial work with lower paying service work. The chart also leads us to dismiss any idea that we had to withdraw because fewer Americans were either willing or able to work. Quite the contrary, total employment has risen explosively. Today a significantly higher proportion of Americans work than worked in 1952. The same Federal Reserve data reveals that in 1952, 58% of Americans had non-farm employment. Today, the proportion is 64%, and of course the population is much larger.[3] It also follows that the trends in employment are not caused by rising wealth. Rising wealth might result in falling labor force participation, as the newly prosperous decided to kick off the burdens and drudgery of work. Quite possibly if that were to happen, manufacturing employment would fall faster than employment in services, but labor force participation would in any case have to fall, whereas in reality it has grown.[4]

There is, in summary, no way to reconcile the trends in goods-producing and in service-providing employment as being the result of choices by working people. Although real wages have fallen—which means that the buying power of wage income has fallen—there has been a steady erosion in the kinds of work that pay the best and simultaneously an explosion of service work that does not pay as well.[5] No one could seriously claim that this is what working people wanted to happen.

Upward Mobility

Americans are industrious and optimistic in large part because of the freedom we have to improve our wealth and station. Yet we are no longer leaders in mobility. A recent study concluded that in fact Americans now trail most other advanced economies in this respect.[6] The authors highlighted one notable comparison: between America and Denmark. Their finding was that there is greater opportunity in Denmark for one to rise in wealth and status than there is in America.

The average wage of persons who engage in manufacturing—an average that encompasses not only line workers but product designers, engineers, and technicians of many different kinds—is high in part because of the skill level involved. If a nation is not going to manufacture many things, it does not need product designers, process engineers, industrial test laboratories, or metallurgists. Behind the factory that makes things is another industry whose products are How To make things and What Different Things to make. The demand for the provider of capabilities is derived from the industries that use those capabilities. They are interdependent, and losing either one necessarily results in losing the other also.

There is another statistic that brings home this proposition. In America today there are approximately four and a half million men of middle age—forty to sixty years—who were once working at well paying jobs but are now not employed. Some of them have spent time in prison, but that is only a fraction. The vast majority worked while young at good paying jobs, but the jobs and employers disappeared, leaving these men without gainful employment. Most are unmarried and subsist on welfare and disability insurance. The rest are married, and their wives work to supplement their small income. These men are no longer treated as unemployed because they are not looking for work, but by any sensible definition of unemployment they are unemployed. They are capable of work that would support them and their families, but that kind of work is not available in their area. Were it not for the dole, they would have to move in search of work, but they can get by without work, and so they constitute a new addition to the welfare underclass. They have been discarded. If they were counted as unemployed, the rate of unemployment would be close to nine percent. Since we ignore them, the rate is reported under five percent.

Today vast numbers of people come here from all over the world to look for work. America has always been a magnet for them, but today even more so than at any time in the last century. Whether they come legally or not, they are all upwardly mobile people, which is in itself a good thing as far as it goes, but the end result of substituting foreign workers for native workers is that we have in effect exported our upward mobility. Chinese and Zambians are upwardly mobile by the very fact of having moved to America, but Americans are not. The end result is that in effect we systematically discriminate against American men. To sharpen the point a bit, the worst losers in the process are black men. They have the least upward mobility, according to the report cited above, and the highest rate of non-employment. American men in general and black men especially are simply being discarded.

Wage Trends and Their Causes

The consequences for the working class are dramatic. I summarized some disturbing trends in income growth and in inequality. A more detailed look at wage rates reinforces and expands on them. The data for this following chart comes from the Economic Policy Institute,[7] and is provided by them free of charge. It deals with average wages for men and women, as a function of education. The trend is unmistakable, that since 1973, wages of blue collar men have fallen in real terms—in terms of what their pay will actually buy—while the wages of college graduates, and even more so those of men with post-graduate schooling, have risen in real terms.

The pay of men with less than a high school diploma has fallen about 25% since 1973, while the pay of men with college education has risen about 15%. The men who

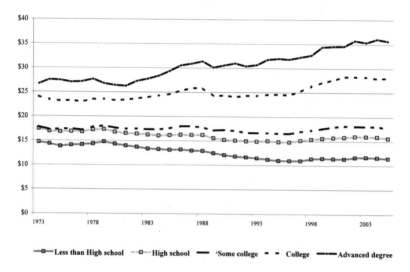

Mens' Real Hourly Wages, by Education
2005 Dollars

—□—Less than High school   ⸱⸱□⸱⸱High school   ■■■ 'Some college   ■ ■ College   ▬▬Advanced degree

Source: Economic Policy Institute and Logistic Research & Trading Co.

used to make things have seen their wages fall. The only blue collar occupation that has drawn in more workers is construction, but even there wages have fallen in real terms. The connection with the trade deficit—a topic I will visit shortly—is unmistakable.

The trends in pay for women ratify this picture. Their wages have risen relative to men. Even the pay of women who have not finished high school has at least held up. Whereas in the past women with little education earned far less than men with similarly little education, at the present time the wage differential of women and men is almost uniform: regardless of education, women are paid between 20% and 25% less than men. This differential, by the way, is not a sign of discrimination. Today, working

20

men put in on average about 43 hours per week at work while women on average work about 28 hours per week. The pay rate of women is an average of full time and part time wages. The "average" woman is a part time worker.[8] Whether any part of the differential reflects discrimination remains open to research; numerous econometrics studies have essentially dismissed the discrimination claim entirely. In any case, the understandable gap between full time and part time wage rates could easily account for the whole "gap." The larger point however is this: to the extent that the increase in full time employment for women explains the rising wages of women, then the real trends in wages offered to women in similar situations are the same as the trends for men. Working class women have fared no better than working class men: their real wages have fallen substantially over the last thirty-five years. The only "gender gap" is that unlike men, women have been able to compensate by working longer hours.

The Trade Deficit: "We Think and They Sweat"

The growing trade deficit—as worrisome as it is by itself—is sometimes invoked in a way that obscures the implications of these wage trends. Everyone knows that our deficit in products—the things that working class men used to make and that white collar men used to invent and design—is disastrous. Many commentators rush however to dismiss trade in products as an artifact of "old" economics. They point out that we run a trade surplus in services. What is less well known, and what they do not stop to explain, is that our trade in services is

21

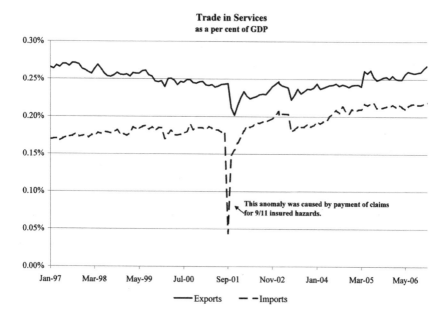

Trade in Services
as a per cent of GDP

This anomaly was caused by payment of claims for 9/11 insured hazards.

——— Exports   — — Imports

Source: Department of Commerce and Logistic Research & Trading Co.

headed the same way as our trade in products. Where we once enjoyed a large trade surplus in services, that surplus has shrunk dangerously. If the present trends were to continue, it would not be long before we are running a deficit in service trade! This proposition, which would probably be rejected as scandalous in many quarters, can be documented by the trade data itself, which comes from the Department of Commerce. The trend over the last decade in trade in services follows.

Ten years ago, our trade surplus in services accounted for about 0.1% of GDP. This is by no means a king's ransom. In dollars it was about $8 billion per year. Today, a decade later, it is half of that as a per cent of GDP: about 0.05% of GDP. In dollars, the surplus has shrunk to $5 billion per year. Total trade in services has grown considerably over that time, so that as a per cent of the gross trade our surplus has shrunk even more. We simply are not a dominant world leader in services any more. It would take only a small further decline to turn our remaining surplus into a deficit. As an example, one of the largest single components of "trade" in services is purchase of insurance. When a German family buys life insurance from Prudential, their premiums are recognized as the dollar value of an export of insurance services. The insurance business today, however, is increasingly dominated by German, Germano-Swiss, and Japanese insurers. Insurance Services is no longer our net export. If the present trend continues it will become just another item in the trade deficit.

There is a slick sound bite making the rounds that says, "We think, they sweat," meaning that American's comparative economic advantage is in creative and complicated thinking and its products, while the strong backs of the rest of the world do the hard labor. Would that it were so. It is far easier to export thinking than sweat, because thinking doesn't weigh anything. There is a new advertising campaign for Toyota, in which they proudly point out that today there are ten Toyota assembly plants located all across America. The men and women who find work there and the men and women who are driving the excellent cars that emerge from those plants have good reason to be thankful, but the lesson is not, "we think, they sweat." On the contrary, the lesson of the Toyota advertising campaign is "we sweat (here in Indiana), while they think (in Tokyo)" about innovative new cars.

In the area of services, where our surplus is disappearing, the largest component of our export of services is financial services. When a foreign institution buys stock

23

on the New York Stock Exchange, the commission it pays is recorded as an export of services. If the same foreign institution approaches a Wall Street firm to put together a complex package of assets—for instance a swap or derivative contract—the huge fees earned by Wall Street are again credited as an export of services, and the ideas and knowledge to create these contracts is true thinking, although the foreign customer is hardly sweating. We have a head start in financial innovation, but that advantage is rapidly disappearing. As foreign stock and bond markets grow, their capability to launch high-tech financial services based on those markets grows explosively. The personnel—the ones who are actually doing the thinking—will also be available over there, because the enrollment at our graduate programs that train the experts in financial technology are overwhelmingly foreign students.

No conceit is more dangerous, and no conceit is surer to be corrected painfully, than the proposition that we, or any single nation, have a comparative advantage when it comes to thinking. Everyone thinks.

The moral of this story is that even the strong wage growth in wages of the most highly educated Americans is not secure. In the following chapter I will take a further look at the high growth rate of the most highly educated, but one central fact is already evident in the preceding charts. To the extent that their compensation is justified by American leadership in technology, that justification will come increasingly under attack. The field of financial engineering, mentioned above, illustrates the broader tends. This is the high tech branch of the finance industry, and of course it was pioneered in America. It is still true that the new professionals are mostly trained here, but very few of them are Americans. At the present time, the largest group seems to be Chinese, with Russian and Brazilian students not far behind.

Not only is our surplus of trade in services shrinking rapidly, it is in any case very small. Even at 0.1% of GDP—the high end of the range of the last decade—it is too small to have a significant effect on the national economy. In order to grow GDP by one per cent it would be necessary to expand the surplus by ten times in a single year! Realistically, even assuming that we think faster than other people, the best one could hope for is that trade in services could add perhaps 0.05% to GDP each year, or about $6 billion. That is only a small fraction of Wal-Mart's annual sales.

Notes

1. See the entry "Human Capital," by Gary S. Becker, in the Concise Encyclopedia of Economics, published on the Web by the Library of Economics and Liberty, 2006. See also his seminal work: Gary Becker. *Human Capital.* New York, National Bureau of Economic Research. 1964. For more recent citations please consult the Journal of Economic Literature, under the heading Human Capital.
2. Board of Governors of the Federal Reserve Board: The Survey of Consumer Finances 2004, prepared by Brian K. Bucks, Arthur B. Kennickell, and Kevin B. Moore. Board of Governors, Washington, DC, 2004.
3. The decline of the farm population—the exodus of farmers from the land—would modify these statistics by raising the proportion of Americans with gainful employment, and would raise it much more in 1952 than today. In practice however farming is a kind of manufacturing, so adding back the farm population would actually deepen the disparity between the trends in "goods production" and in service occupations.
4. The decline of farm employment has had a dramatic impact on American life. It is the source of the massive shift of the African-American population out of the Deep South and into the urban North. It has at the same time aggravated chronic unemployment, because those who mi-

grated north were in many cases unable to secure work, and became dependent on the welfare state where they have remained trapped in welfare dependency and underemployment.

5. Quite obviously there are many service jobs that pay extremely well, including for instance brain surgery. I will return to this point later, but simply taking into account the number of such jobs, it is very clear that they do not begin to explain the expansion of the service sector.

6. Thomas Hertz. Understanding Mobility in America. The Center for American Progress; Washington, D.C. April 2006.

7. See the web site, www.epinet.org. Their own analysis of the conditions of working Americans, covering many aspects besides wage rates, can be found in their book: The State of Working America 2006/2007. The Economic Policy Institute: Washington, D.C. 2006.

8. In 1979, the "average" working women worked less than 20 hours per week. The wage differential has compressed principally because more women are full time employees today.

3
Education Today

We as a nation profess a commitment to universal education—indeed the whole world does so today.[1] Universal education is a precondition for both upward mobility and for productive labor and high wages. It is an education that provides every person with the opportunity to learn at least the basics of skills and knowledge that will serve him throughout life. There is no expectation that all the people will master them equally. Our more modest goal must be to insure that however differently two persons grow to be, the differences are not ones that we created but that emerged spontaneously and naturally from the persons themselves. Entire volumes have been devoted to the subject of American public education, though the payoff from this effort has yet to be realized. I can only recommend that every American get informed and get involved. Education is too important to leave to the self-serving "educators." Discrimination against American men starts in the schools, as one little factoid illustrates. In the past, boys consistently scored higher than girls on the SAT test, but now their scores are essentially equal. The girls' scores did not rise; the boys' scores fell. What price equality?

There is in the end only one educational reform than can make a difference, and that is to privatize all schools.

Why are any schools in America actually run by local government? We taught the world that the government has a duty to use our taxes to guarantee to all children the chance to get the education they need to succeed. All schools should be supported by public money, and in most of the world that is the case. Only here do they deny tax money to a class of schools—private and parochial—that provide education to the children. But what is the link from financial support to management and dictation? Our local educational bureaucracy is simply incompetent and unwilling or unable to educate the children. We have what is in fact a gigantic Soviet school system in which no one is responsible, no one has the power or authority to bring about reform, and the status continues to slide from quo to low.[2] There is no reform without privatization, and that is just as true of our schools as it was for the Soviet economy. There is no alternative to placing the authority to make decisions in the hands of those who, by being closest to the children, have the greatest stake in the results of their decisions.

Privatization simply means that each and every school—kindergarten through twelfth grade—would operate as a private school. Schools could be permitted to join together, but not locally. In the interests of choice, the schools in an area that serve the same population—e.g. competing junior high schools—must be independent of each other. Each school would be accountable to the children and to their parents, because there would be complete freedom of choice.

The state would have two important functions. First, it would provide financial support in the form of a voucher for every pupil, sufficient to cover the education that our laws guarantee to every child. The voucher must be uniform for all children of a given grade.[3] Second, the state is required to fix minimum criteria for coverage of subjects and minmal performance criteria for promotion and certification. Setting these standards is by no means an infringement on the schools. It serves the same guarantee of universal education as the universal vouchers do. If the state has a duty to provide universal education, it must necessarily first define universal education. The schools would be free to exceed the minima, just as they would be free to raise income from other sources besides the state. They would also be free to teach other subjects, as long as those subjects do not violate the law or promote anti-social behavior. Catholic schools could teach Catholic doctrine, Muslim schools Islamic doctrine, and secular humanist schools secular doctrine, but no school would be permitted to teach methods of strangling one's neighbors to death. Note that under these rules there could be no whining that the state is "paying Muslim schools to teach Islam." The state is paying the cost of the guaranteed universal education.[4] If any school wants to offer additional subject matter, it is their problem to pay for it. The local educational bureaucracy would be tasked to supervise the schools to insure that they are true to their duty.

Higher Education

The deficiencies of American education are not confined to the elementary and high schools. Colleges and graduate school also have their problems, though they are very different. The college and university "industry" is entirely privatized, which goes to show that privatization alone—decentralizing the direction of schools—is not a panacea. While there are problems with the operations of our universities however, I have no ready formula to improve them. The vagueness of intellectual standards—or in many cases the near absence of standards—found there may be inevitable consequences of the freedom that higher education requires. It is better to address the failings of a particular school or program individually, avoiding blanket, one-size-fits-all "solutions."

The case of the fradulent "Professor" Churchill of the University of Colorado is a case in point. Fire him, certainly. The refusal to fire him would signal a broader flaw in his university, and of course the granting of tenure already raises questions, but the way to address this scandal is at the individual level. I would add, as a sidelight, that he has no defense on grounds of intellectual freedom. Universities and colleges exist to serve the students. Every professor is free to serve his students but is not free to cheat them of education. The professor is an employee of the university and as such his only right is the right to be paid for his services. If what he provides is not a service but a disservice, he is left with no rights at all viz-a-vis the university or its students. None of this vitiates in any way the right to free speech, to free inquiry, and to free conscience that are the birthright of every person.[5]

There is however one common aspect of American higher education that represents a failure to ensure educational opportunity to Americans. On every college campus American boys are scarce—representing about 35% of all American students—and foreign students are numerous. As a rule the foreign students are quite good, and one would have to say that as a nation we are lucky to have them. The fact remains however that we are systematically replacing American boys with foreign boys and girls (it is my impression that among foreign students, boys and girls are about equal in numbers). The ratio of girls to boys is not in any way unique to America. It is close to the norm all over the world. The principal reason for it is that nearly all careers for women require a college diploma, while men have their choice of many excellent careers that do not demand any college. It is not necessarily a sign that unfair handicaps are put in the path of education for boys, but in practice discrimination against boys is evident in the disparate performance of boys and girls on standardized tests. That tilt has already been in force since grammar school. Whatever the situation of boys versus girls in American colleges, the substitution of foreign for native students in colleges is in any case another matter.

For a foreign student, the chance to attend college in America is the chance not only to emigrate, but to enter the new society among the privileged. Berths in our universities are plums doled out by our government in exchange for favors granted by other—usually third world—governments. When the president visits Ecuador, he brings amongst other things places at our universities as consideration to compensate for commercial or political or military favors they bestow on us. In addition to the immediate payoff to us, the natural tie between the two countries that comes from having a ruling class educated here represents a lasting fund of good will. If it did not come at the cost of excluding our own people from our universities, it would be an unambiguous good.[6]

While the number of foreign undergraduates is comparatively small, the number of foreign graduate students is enormous. In all the sciences and engineering specialties, and in most or all the social sciences, American graduate students account for a minority, and generally a small minority, of graduate students. Of all doctorates in economics granted each year, American students represent about ten percent of the total. A surprising number—probably more than ten percent—come from Brazil alone. But the places in our graduate schools are widely distributed across the whole world.[7] As a natural result, teaching faculties at all colleges and universities are becoming increasingly dominated by foreign professors too. That simply could not happen without discrimination against American students, and especially American men. One of the signs of discrimination, as explained by Gary Becker,[8] is that the victim class are found amongst the top performers in their field, but are suspiciously missing amongst the large body of average performers. Discrimination can not make the ordinary brilliant, but it can keep the ordinary majority of the victim class disappear in favor of the ordinary majority of the discriminators. That aptly describes doctoral studies in America today, and increasingly it describes the faculties of American colleges and universities.

Many of the foreign-born faculty are leaders in their fields and wise and learned professors. But most share a common trait that pulls them in the direction of compromising on the education they deliver. On campuses all over the country, it is obvious that the good will and approval of the students is a necessity for success as a teacher. This always presents an inducement to compromise the product, an inducement that tugs at both American and foreign-born faculty. The foreign-born are however especially susceptible to it. If an American professor loses his job because of hostility from the students, he has to get another job, but if a foreign-born professor loses his job he may very well have to go home. Even if he is a citizen by that time, if no appealing alternative presents itself he can retreat to the safety and support available in his home country. But why risk having to beat a shameful retreat? The answer presents itself as if unbidden.

Discrimination always means that advancement is not based solely on merit. It always means that opportunity is not open equally to all. That is especially intolerable when the victims are American people, because of the promise of help and support that America, and every nation, owes to its native citizens. We are, to reiterate a point above, exporting our upward mobility to buy favors and good will from other countries and from their ruling classes. The young men and women who come here looking for education and opportunity were not, after all, drawn from the poor and marginalized people in their home lands. They are the privileged class; offspring of the people who we wish to appease all over the world.

Immigration

Immigration is one of the defining issues in America today.[9] Unlike my remarks above, the public debate is focused on illegal immigration. In terms of numbers, there is no question that illegal immigration is a problem, and it is a problem that arouses deep and genuine emotions. If America is going to be a functioning community, the people must see that the men and women they elect are working for the common good of that community. The torrent of illegal immigration and the obvious indifference of our elected leaders—"indifference" being perhaps a too kind word for the reaction—casts doubt amongst the public. Nonetheless, illegal immigration does not represent the sort of problem that we are addressing here. It would be possible for it to enhance the productivity and welfare

33

of the American people, and that is the topic of this small book.

The immigration that is not enhancing our productivity, but that causes our fellow citizens to be left behind and their ambitions thwarted, is primarily legal immigration. This is not to say that legal immigration, including the immigration path that comes through our colleges, universities, and graduate schools, is entirely bad. It brings many individuals who contribute greatly to our life and communities. It is not however all to the good, because it substitutes for native development.

What should we do? Simple. We have to make sure that our own children are prepared to the best of their talents and abilities to succeed and achieve. We have to stop the dream machine and stand for accountability and choice in their education. Along the way it would not hurt to advertise good examples of achievement and upward mobility. After we have done the spade work of instilling accountability and healthy ambition up through twelfth grade, we have to extend it through college too. The vast variety of subjects that a university offers, and the extreme diversity of programs that the students follow makes any kind of simple "standards" program unfeasible. Still, it is necessary to address grade inflation somehow. The way to fix standards of performance that does work in English Lit and neurobiology both is to communicate to all the faculty that in every field there are absolute standards of performance. Each field of study should take it upon themselves to establish and to teach canons of performance for their field which would be taught to all faculty and which all faculty would be expected to enforce. After all, how can a professor of English Lit or a professor of neurobiology, claiming to be an expert in his or her field, refuse to recognize and implement the common standards that his peers have established?

I do not know much about English Lit or neurobiology, but I can offer a simple example from one that I know something about, statistics. After a student has taken college statistics, what does he actually know, and how well can he perform? One of the basic building blocks of statistics is called "correlation." I would propose that no one should get "A" marks in statistics unless he understands what correlation signifies, when and how to use it, and its reliability. That, to pursue this single example, is what an "A" means in statistics. No one should get an "A" unless he or she meets that standard. No A's for effort. No A's because of how far the student has come from his lowly beginnings. No A's because he needs these credits to keep his scholarship. A's for those who—in a preliminary way because in this example we are only talking about the first college course—understand the essentials of statistics. It is the responsibility of the leaders in each field of study to make the myriad judgments of what is an "A," what is a "B," and so on and to publish the resulting standards for all to see. It is moreover their responsibility to see to it that these standards are taught in graduate school, to all the next generation of faculty. It is not necessary for them to assign letter grades to different competencies. It would be enough to recognize conceptual categories of "excellence," "competence," "adequacy" and so on.

Then, since all the faculty of any field of study, statistics, neurobiology or English Lit, at a given college have accepted and endorsed the standards of their profession, it would be possible for them to question the basis on which any single one of their faculty give grades. Not in a hostile or aggressive way. I do not want to reinstitute the

Inquisition. But in a meaningful practical way, because there really is no science of neurobiology unless the neurobiologists themselves can set down on paper a canon of standards for what it means to be one of them, and by the same token there really is no science of neurobiology unless the practitioners accept that canon as binding on their personal judgments. This canon can never be set in stone. It has to be a guide. That is the difference between grammar school, where the canons, are quite clear and precise—permitting the school to use objective testing methods—and graduate school. In the latter, the students and faculty are both operating on the frontiers of their field, and they cannot work with "the Standards Committee" peering inquisitively over their shoulders or breathing down their necks. What we have in college today however is the opposite. It is a failure to define education; an unwillingness to set standards. Notwithstanding my cautious qualifiers above, I hold that once a canon has been fixed within a field of study, it is the task of every faculty member nationwide to be able to demonstrate that he is faithfully implementing them.

Summary

This chapter raises the question of whether Americans are doing the right—the must useful and productive—things. The evidence that we are on the whole not doing what we are capable of lies in the widening gap between rich and poor and in the falling real wages of American workers. These trends can in large part be tied to the demise of manufacturing in America. They can also be tied to the failure of education in America, in both the public schools system and at the college level.

Notes

1. For the most part this truly is the result of our example. But before we injure ourselves with self-congratulation, we should acknowledge that it was the Catholic Church that introduced universal education, in Charlemagne's Holy Roman Empire. He decreed, and the Church delivered, education to all children of the empire. Our parochial schools systems—primarily Catholic, Lutheran, and Episcopal—survive to document this noble heritage.

2. Our schools seem to have substituted flattery—grade inflation and feel-good moments—in place of education. Evidence of this comes from a study reported in the journal *Social Problems*. The authors surveyed thousands of high school seniors, comparing their expressed career ambitions against the actual achievement of comparable youths. The seniors whose dreams they had before them were clearly unrealistic. See Reynolds, Stewart, MacDonald, and Sischo, "Have Adolescents Become Too Ambitious? High School Seniors' Educational and Occupational Plans, 1976 to 2000," *Social Problems,* 53(2), May 2006, p. 186–206. In nearly every school's office, it seems, there is as multicolored poster on the wall that greets visitors with a legend saying something like "The Dream starts here." Apparently we have too much dreaming and not enough achieving.

3. There can be no exception to this rule, except perhaps to cover actual, documentable expenses of handicapped children: e.g. hearing aids or eye glasses. The budget for vouchers has to be set high enough to provide for the universal education of any child. The fact that today there is more generous support for various classes of so-called "special needs" children only provides a corrupting incentive to assign children to that category, for which the expenses are high and the expectations are rock bottom.

4. For the state to refuse to recognize schools because they teach religious ideas is of course a blatant persecution of religion, in contravention of the Bill of Rights.

5. I write this after having taught at various universities for seventeen years, ranging from the community college to the University of Chicago, and having exercised my god-given right to these freedoms for many more years than that.

6. The United States is by no means the only country that woos foreign students for political purposes. All major countries do it, and China is probably the most visibly active in this effort right now.

7. About fifteen years ago I was asked by a colleague who happened to be the Midwest chief of the Office of Naval Research to help him find an adjutant. The candidate should be a young scientist and an American citizen, because he would have to enlist in the Navy. I began my search at my alma mater, Northwestern University, in the department of mathematics. They had about thirty-six young assistant professors in the department. They turned out however to be not such a promising source, because only one of the thirty-six was American! The others came from

all over, with no more than two from any single country. Americans, it seems, are uniquely unable to master higher math. That of course is not really true; Americans are as smart as other people. It just seems to be true.

8. Gary Becker. *The Economics of Discrimination.* U of Chicago Press: Chicago, Ill. 1957. 2nd ed. 1971.

9. 2006.

4

An Application:
Begging for Poverty

It is said that a cynic knows the cost of everything, but the value of nothing. That is the formula for poverty.

As important as formal education is, it alone is neither a necessary nor a sufficient basis for effectiveness and ultimately for wealth. The very best education can enable a person to become a highly productive and highly paid employee, but by itself it does not guarantee that he will actually be effective in life. It is always possible for even the highest paid laborer to fritter away the wages he is paid, and at heart to remain wedded to poverty and dependence. It is for that reason that efforts to promote industry in third world countries, while these efforts are laudable in themselves, do not automatically break the cycle of poverty that is so endemic there. What separates the first and third worlds is not only learned skills. What separates them is a culture of productivity, a culture of efficiency.

The effective man or woman is the person who is always asking himself "Why am I doing this? What should I be doing now?" The wise Peter Drucker once described a valued employee as a person who does things right, and an effective manager as one who does the right things.[1]

The worker works efficiently because he implements the tasks that are assigned to him and expected of him. The manager however works at a higher level of effectiveness because he chooses the most valuable tasks to devote himself to. Effectiveness can, like everything else, be learned at least to some extent. It does not seem however to be learned in school. The most famous executive today, who is also the richest, is Bill Gates of Microsoft Corporation. He dropped out of college in order to devote his time and energy to pursuing what he did best. This is not to diminish the importance of education, as evidence the fact that the vast majority of his employees are highly educated, but it makes the point that effectiveness is not itself a college subject.

On Begging and the Value of Time

Even in the most advanced and modern societies, public begging and panhandling are a fact of life. Some people, it seems, will always be beggars. The scale of begging however is vastly different between rich and poor communities. Begging moreover is only one manifestation of a way of life that is widely practiced in poor places. When we visit such places we wonder why the local people are not ashamed to beg, as we are, and while we feel human empathy for them, we are secretly grateful for our manifest superiority.

Begging is not shameful. Saint Francis of Assisi was a beggar, and he required his followers to support themselves by begging. In this way they delivered the message of how they identified with the poor and of how we should all look beyond present comfort and wealth. That is something we would all do well to learn, but unfortunately one has to actually be poor to teach it. Saint Francis was a model of effectiveness. He just didn't turn his product into gold, as the rest of us are inclined to do. He lived a millennium ago, but we are surrounded with more current examples of honorable begging. Churches beg, as do NPR radio stations. The alma mater and the symphony and the Salvation Army beg too. We are given many opportunities to make choices about how we should use our money, even if in doing so we do not derive any immediate value. Yet we instinctively and wisely regret the widespread begging in poor countries.

What is wrong with begging then? The poor, it seems, beg because they are poor. There is nothing "wrong" with being poor. It is not immoral or wicked in itself. What then is wrong when the poor resort to begging?

What is wrong is this. The poor—and to repeat a comment above, there will always be some poor beggars; the issue here is with a sort of culture of begging that pervades a poor place—do not beg because they are poor. They are poor because they beg. If they stopped begging they would not become miraculously rich, but they could become a lot less poor. Beyond the rather immediate payoff, moreover, they would be launched on a learning process that I referred to above as a culture of efficiency. The poor beg because they have nothing more useful to do with their time, or because they *think* they have nothing more important to do with their time. They continue to beg because they really are not aware of how much their time is worth, and have not given much thought to what else they could be doing. Their poverty tends to be hereditary because their parents and their neighbors have likewise not thought very deeply about how they could and should be devoting their time, and so the individual does not receive much enlightenment or counsel from either parents or neighbors that could lead to more fulfilling lives.

Begging and many other time-wasting practices that are very prevalent in poor countries are the functional equivalent of laziness. The poor for their part think that they are working hard because their toil is ceaseless. In rural China, it is normal for a farmer to harvest a small quantity of his crop in the morning, then to load his goods in a cart that he pulls behind his rickety bicycle and take off for the nearest town, where he spends the afternoon sitting patiently on the sidewalk waiting for passers-by to buy his goods. The trip by bicycle alone must be exhausting in such a hilly country. Yet even the most extreme physical exertions are the functional equivalent of laziness. The problem is that the real value of the time that he spends is far greater than the meager reward in money terms. He is spending a dollar's worth of time to receive a dime in cash. No wonder he is poor!

To continue with the example of rural China, the problem is that his traditional way of life has confused money with value. The value of what he could be accomplishing is larger than the money that he earns. There is a lot of free land available on the hillsides—land that the government does not regulate and that is therefore free—and farmers do extend their cultivation up the hills. That takes time and back-breaking effort to do, but it is a better use of his time than sitting on a sidewalk waiting for the townspeople to buy a melon from him. The answer is not to berate the farmer. He needs money because it is a unique good: one that he can exchange for all the things he cannot produce for himself. The way to improve the farmer's lot is not to lecture him; or even less to accuse him of laziness. The key is to build around him a marketing infrastructure that relieves him of the necessity of selling his crop one melon at a time. There should be a buyer who makes the rounds of the farm villages in his truck, buying up the produce and conveying it to a network of wholesale and retail grocery outlets. Then the farmer would be free to spend his time and energy on being a better farmer, and he would have cash money to use as needed. I am confident, moreover, that this is the direction that rural China will take, and that this infrastructure is developing right now.

This example however applies in many contexts, including begging. All of them arise from confusing money with value, and they occur because the poor simply are unaware of the true value of their time. The Nobel Peace Prize for 2006 went to Yunus Mohammed, who invented what he calls "micro loans" that can lift the poor out of their poverty. The genius of the micro loan is that it suspends for a brief time that link between immediate production and immediate cash available. The poor are freed from the financial treadmill that keeps them expending dollars of potential created value in order to scrape for pennies. They cannot realize that value alone, however, because it exists in a broader social and economic framework. The poor beggar would probably be better off simply cleaning and improving his simple home than cadging for nickels, and he could do that on his own, but like all of us he needs money, and only an economic context can consistently turn value into cash.

Free Enterprise

The buyer who shops for farm produce in the villages and the wholesale and retail grocers who ply their trade after him do so to make a profit. They want to have as much money left over for them, after expenses, as possible. Their reward is not calibrated to the hours they work, but is directly linked to value they create. The self interest that draws them into those professions and every other kind of occupation—even the infinite variety of occupations that no one has even imagined up to this time—acts like a magnet to align money with value.

The monetized economy is one in which anything can be exchanged for—and in effect converted into—anything else. Everything has a price which both rewards the few enterprises who provide that thing, and that limits the desires of the many who want to have some of it. In the ideal economy, it seems to be unnecessary to dig deeper in order to identify value, to assess value directly, because the entrepreneurial profession closes the gap between value and money value. We can simply take the money price of anything as being its value. This is only an ideal of course. In practice we do have to dig deeper and to know more. But most of all, it is the entrepreneurs who make this work. They find what is of large value but some cost; they acquire or build it at cost; and then resell it for its value.

Note

1. Peter F. Drucker. *The Effective Executive: the Definitive Guide to Getting the Right Things Done.* HarperCollins Publishers, in their HarperBusiness series. 2006. This is a revised version of a classic essay on management.

5

Cheap Capital

Capital is a unique contributor to the creation of economic value. Its uniqueness consists in the fact that while it must work cooperatively with the other contributors, it is deaf, dumb, and unconscious. All those decisions about how, when, and where to employ a given bit of knowledge or a sophisticated tool have to be made by some person, an actual human being, who has a right to profit from the fruits of whatever the tool produces. The existence of inanimate, and largely immaterial, capital necessitates Management, to negotiate on its behalf. Very often, some laborer possesses some key capital, which is inseparable from his own work. Capital goods however are often so large and costly that the laborers could not possibly afford to own them, and in this case the Capitalist is a distinct kind of worker, whose contribution comes not from direct production work but from the indirect labor of managing the way his capital is used. This description of productive work lacks only one clause to make it more recognizable in practical terms. That last ingredient is that it is usually easier for the laborers to adapt what they do to the peculiarities of the capital rather than the other way around. For capital and labor to function together effectively it is generally necessary for the capitalist to manage not only his unique property, but to manage and direct labor too. This is particularly clear in the case of the capital that consists of the reputation and name recognition of the product and the company that makes it, which is to say its franchise.

Small capital assets serve individuals, households, and small business, and in all cases the premise of "capitalism," which is to permit almost unlimited freedom to individuals to acquire and use capital, is the reality. Larger and larger assets however progressively lose their private character in America today. Milton Friedman, who was not only an eminent economist but was also one of the chief philosophers of freedom, noted recently that when he was young—during the 1930's—the air was filled with talk of socialism, while the reality of America was *laissez-faire,* but now though the air is filled with paeans of praise to freedom and *laissez-faire,* the reality is socialism. In this chapter I will document the degree of political control of business at the highest levels and of the institutions that were formed to facilitate *laissez-faire* capitalism. And more importantly, perhaps, I will make the case that the toll is high to the productivity of business. I call this chapter "Cheap Capital," because our corporate titans can thrive only in a world of cheap—that is to say, subsidized—capital. At the outset let me state clearly that this is by no means a uniquely American fault. Just the contrary, America was once the exception in the amount of freedom afforded capitalism, and the indispensable, collateral discipline of failure. In a gradual change that started as recently as the Great Depression our large corporations have been deemed "too big to fail." They now operate in a kind of forced partnership in which the freedom to fail has gone the way of the profit motive.

Cooking the Books of Crony Capitalism

Nowhere is this change more evident than in the ways that corporate management have found to feather their own nests at the expense of the owners, and at the expense of the financial viability of their companies. The outrageous pay of management has been documented elsewhere, adorned with stunning statistics about the exploding pay gap between labor and management. The rogues' gallery of outrageous corporate larceny is long and the walls are crowded with snapshots—including some startlingly familiar ones—but one current example will do for all. I have chosen the example of a homebuilder called NVR, which builds single family homes in Virginia. It is not a small business by any means, having about 5,400 employees as of the 2005 annual report, but it is a dwarf amongst other builders like Centex and Kaufman & Broad.

The corporate officers are paid very well, both in the form of regular salary, annual bonus in cash, and contributions to their retirement plan. The chairman of the board received last year about two million dollars in salary, another two million in cash bonus, and a small contribution to the retirement plan. His compensation in cash amounted to a little more than four million dollars. The top management are reported to have been paid collectively about seven million dollars. For a company that reported a profit of about $700 million in 2005, that is generous but not outrageous.[1] The central, unanswered question is however whether they actually earned $700 million in 2005, and whether in fact they had any profits at all. One sign that in fact they had no profits is that, as in every previous year, they paid no dividends to the shareholders. Thus, while the company had profits of, allegedly, $700 million, the investors had profits of zero.

The very large obstacle that looms between reported profits and visible profits is made of stock options to the management. Over the last ten years, the chairman of the board has been issued options on more than 790,000 shares. We do not know—it is not reported—what is the average strike of those options, so we can not attach a dollar value, but the value would have to be close to a half billion dollars. The directors and executives of the company have all received options, and the annual report does provide information on the strikes embedded in those options in aggregate. As of the end of 2005, there were outstanding options on 3,080,000 shares. In addition, over the three years from 2003 to 2005, the management had exercised options on a total of about one and a half million shares. Since the shares peaked at around $950 per share in 2005, it is almost certain that the options they exercised were worth, say, $500 each. That is a total of $750,000,000 dollars paid out by the corporation to its management over three years; a sum that exceeds the highest profit in any single year by a very large margin. During those three years, NVR reported a total profit of about $1,640 million, but that does not reflect the cost of the options that were exercised. Deducting the cost of the options, profits for the three years were $930 million. The cost of the options exercised in those recent years consumed about 45% of reported profits. This moreover neglects the cost of additional, unexercised options granted in those years.

As of the end of 2005, as noted above, there were outstanding options on slightly more than three million shares. We are able to assess their market value because the option strikes are reported in the annual report.

Using the price per share as of today,[2] $545, outstanding options are worth more than $910 million. Deducting this cost from the reported profits of the last three years, we are left with $930 million minus $910 million, or $20 million dollars. So, let's tally it up; of the $1,640 million that NVR claims to have earned from 2003 through 2005, $1,620 million went to the management and $20 million are left for the investors. The investors would probably have consoled themselves with a $20 million dollar dividend, but the management in its wisdom deemed that a foolish and wasteful outlay of hard-earned cash.[3]

It comes as no surprise that after peaking at $950, shares of NVR fell in 2006 to a low of $385 per share. Since the company doesn't actually have any profits, and since even their phantom reported profits are predicted to fall deeply this year and next, $385 per share seems more than generous to us. But who can account for markets! The shares are now back to $545 per share. Who is paying $545—no doubt on its way back to $950—for worthless stock? No one who invests in the hope of making money. I will return to this point: only players who don't care about making money would invest in this company.[4]

So, with apologies for singling out the eminent men of NVR, this is how corporate America works today. It brought us the bubble and crash of 2000, and will bring us the next crash too. The next bubble is already here.

Manipulated Markets

It comes as no surprise that markets do crazy things. We mere mortals think of ourselves as paragons of rationality, and to a degree we are. We never deliberately shoot ourselves in the foot. No, it always comes as a complete surprise when our feet start to bleed painfully. But when a lot of us get together and let our collective ignorance out of the cage, we wind up doing things that no single one would ever think of doing. If, therefore, I am going to criticize our markets for commodities and for financial assets, it is not enough to point out peculiar and inexplicable events. Those can happen quite naturally. The evidence that counts toward my thesis consists of peculiar but highly explicable events. The story of NVR shares is this kind of evidence. The shares are literally worthless, but at the moment they are rallying straight up. Peculiar indeed, but what is the explanation?

It is that there are many institutions, wielding collectively far more money than mere investors do, who are not buying shares to make money. Examples? The Bank of Japan; the Saudi Arabian Finance Authority (i.e. the Saudi central bank); the Singaporean state retirement funds. These are not commercial entities, they are political entities. They buy financial assets when that serves the political interests of the ruling powers and sell them when that is political to do. On an operational basis the political players are supposed to submit to orchestration by the Federal Reserve Board and its chairman. That is not by any means how it always works in practice because international politics is a very fractious business, but whether in harmony or in conflict, the actual investment merits of the assets they buy and sell are of minor importance to them.

The example of NVR, which gets its capital for free, is a revealing insight into how capitalism and capital markets work today, but it needs to be complemented by indicators that span the whole capital markets. Thus we turn our attention from the individual, NVR, to interest rates that factor into every investment decision and thus to the market as a whole.

Real Interest Rates

The Treasury issues bonds and notes of many different maturities up to thirty years. The whole bundle of Treasury debt constitutes the official National Debt, although the true national debt also includes debt incurred by many different agencies of the government besides the Treasury. The true national debt is far larger than the Treasury debt, but what the Treasury owes is still impressive. The yields on Treasury debt are, moreover, the benchmark against which all other financial assets are measured. While the whole of the national debt figures in the valuation of assets, by far the single most influential figure is the yield of notes that mature in one year, the so-called "Year Bill." If there is any one interest rate that could be called "The" interest rate, it would be the yield on one year Treasury notes.[5] It is, for instance, almost exactly equal to the yield of money market funds. As such, it influences the retail public directly in two ways: as the income they derive from money market balances, and as the cost of taking money from the money market and plunging it into the stock market.

The recent history of the Year Bill shows just how cheap capital is in America. It shows just how heavily capital is subsidized here and how low the hurdle has been set to justify equity investment, business debt, and personal borrowing. There is one adjustment to the Year Bill that sharpens the focus considerably. Whatever funds we lend out today will be repaid tomorrow in dollars that will probably buy less because the cost of living will have risen. Thus the actual income in real terms that we derive from the Year Bill is not the yield itself, but the yield diminished by the inflation we expect. That difference is called in economics the Real Bill. Ordinary interest rates can never be negative numbers because that would mean that we actually accept to be repaid only part of what we lent. We never need to settle for that because we always have the option to keep our money safe at home. The Real Bill however can be negative. Inflation is going to happen no matter what we do individually. So as long as the Year Bill offers some positive yield, we are better taking it than refusing to take it. If the yield does not cover inflation, well that's just too bad. The chart below traces out the history of the Real Bill over the last ten years, 1996–2006.

The long term average of the Real Bill—based on the forty years from 1956 to 1996—is 3%. On average a holder of Year Bills earns enough to cover inflation, plus 3%. The comfortable 3% Real Bill has been missing in action in recent years, and the actual Real Bill has been as low as *minus* 4%! The borrower doesn't pay to take out a loan, he is paid and he has been paid a lot—as much as 4%—to borrow. He expects to pay off his debt in dollars that will be so depreciated that he will have a profit left over even if he simply kept the money tucked away in some form that tracks inflation.

It goes without saying that borrowers have been lining up in droves to take advantage of this bonanza, but that is not the whole story. It is only natural to ask who would be lending on such disadvantageous terms. That question is very easily answered: the money comes from public, government sources and from commercial sources that are in reality subject to the same governments. The most generous benefactor has been Japan, whose domes-

Real Bill

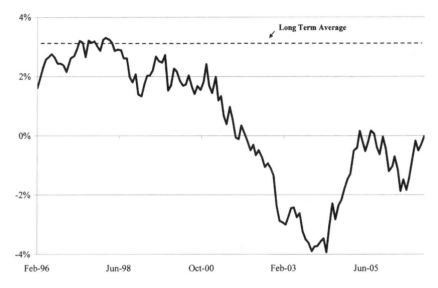

Source: Logistic Research & Trading Co.

tic interest rates are even lower than the Real Bills shown above. The sultans and sheikhs along the Persian Gulf have been almost equally gracious, and China has not stinted either. Why would they lend to us when interest rates are so low that we are in effect stealing directly from them?

One reason is that they do not need to worry about our expected inflation as such. What matters to them is the value in terms of their own money, of the dollars they will receive. Thus for instance, if their own currency is losing value to the dollar, they will be rewarded for keeping their money in American dollars for the year. In point of fact however, the dollar has generally been falling in value since 9/11. The Japanese Yen has been falling even a little faster, so for Japanese lenders there is some profit in lending dollars now, to receive dollars a year later. The rest of the generous world have been seeing the dollars they own—by virtue of owning bonds that pay in dollars—fall in value, further reducing the meager Year Bill yield. Although these calculations based on differential exchange rates are important however, they do not capture the most important consideration.

The one fact that Japan, the Persian Gulf, China, and a lot of other places have in common is that they want to sell us stuff. They are actually addicted to selling us stuff. If however when we buy something from them, they keep the dollars we pay, we would soon be unable to buy any more. The solution is simplicity itself—from the Japanese point of view. When an American pays you for something—a car or a television—lend the money right back to him, so he can afford to buy something else. Don't sell for cash, sell on credit. For more than ten years commentators here and in Japan have puzzled over the seemingly endless Japanese "Recession." There is no mystery however, and there was no recession. Japan is just being impoverished by the policy—mandated by their government—to give us cars that we never pay for. This, by the way, is called "Globalization." So, now we know who the lenders are. The more interesting question remains.

We Americans borrow a lot, but why don't we borrow a hundred times as much? We are being paid to borrow. Is it modesty that prevents us from taking full advantage of the offer? Our borrowing is limited by what we can do with the money we borrow. At the depths of the recent recession the Treasury could have borrowed from Japan and been paid four per cent, in real terms, to do it. Private sector borrowers have to pay higher interest rates than the Treasury, but still the terms of borrowing were very advantageous. Why not borrow more? The reason is simple. You will still borrow only if what you can do with the money is profitable enough to cover the interest. For several years now, the interest has been zero or even negative, but there is no guarantee that an American business could net out a profit even on those easy terms. This is the sticking point. For quite a while, American business has been so unprofitable that it hesitates to borrow virtually free money!

Cheap capital indeed. How cheap does capital have to become—how generously must it be subsidized by the rest of the world—to stimulate borrowing and investing? We have some idea about that, because we Americans, individuals and business, have been borrowing, but only when it is virtually free.

The Politics of Home Mortgage Financing

The preceding section deals with very broad generalities, which are important even when they seem abstract, but those generalities came home in very concrete terms in the summer of 2006. According to data collected by the Federal Reserve Board, household borrowing had decelerated steadily for well over a year, until July, 2006. For the next several months, crucial months in the run up to the mid-term elections, mortgage lending exploded at an unprecedented rate. In May of 2006, outstanding term loans—principally more mortgages and auto loans—amounted to about $1,350 billion. By July it had increased more than ten per cent, to $1,500 billion. Credit card debt also jumped, but by a more modest five per cent. Total household debt expanded in two months by more than eight per cent! Starting in 1945, it had taken about sixty years for debt to grow to where it was in May, and in two months it grew another eight per cent!^{6} To place this further in perspective, in the last couple of years, before last May, the growth rate of household debt was exceptionally low by historical standards, and had been falling for years. The American public had shown a clear preference to at least stop enlarging their debt, but the summer changed that.

The difference that year was exceptionally aggressive selling of new loans, of mortgage refinancing, and of new credit cards and higher credit limits on existing cards. All of a sudden, lending institutions were awash with cash, and it seemed that no American was too high a risk to pass up. The number of annoying phone calls from lending institutions positively exploded. Where did the loanable funds come from? Not from domestic sources, because the Federal Reserve had stuck with its tight money policy. The money came from Japan and China, and from the Persian Gulf where the coffers were bulging with the profits from $60 crude oil and $3 gasoline. These sources represent a slush fund that is always ready to serve the political needs and desires of the American administration. And need it was, because mid-term elections were coming and the American people were demonstrably unhappy. They were so unhappy that, casting gratitude aside, they took control of the Congress from the Republicans and put it in the hands of the Democrats. They refinanced the mortgage, bought a new Japanese car, and then voted against the White House that had made it so easy to borrow.

One of the truly shocking facts about the housing market and mortgage financing is how unprofitable it is. When a sector is growing and presumably successful we naturally expect that success will be rewarded at the bottom line. That, after all, is the whole point of capitalism. I have however already presented the homebuilder NVR as an exhibit of losses where there should be—and where the annual report claims to find—handsome profits. It is not, in that case, that NVR sells its structures below cost. It is merely that whatever they seem to profit from the homes, they pay out to the executives in bonuses. The two grand mortgage lenders—the Federal National Mortgage Association [Fannie Mae] and the Federal Home Loan Board [Freddie Mac]—don't seem to make any money either. In this case, the profits we would expect are simply given as subsidy to the home buyers. In a business sense, mortgage lending is a failure.

The financial details of these two government agencies tell the story, sort of. Fannie Mae stands accused of cooking the books to such an extent that they have been unable to produce reformed, corrected financial reports for the last eighteen months. They have not yet filed an annual report for 2005, and in place of the report there is only a note saying that they now disavow the reports filed in earlier years, and that—presumably—the truth is on its way. As I recall, my sons used to leave notes in the cookie jar too. Freddie Mac, by contrast, tells all. In 2005 they reported a net profit of $2.9 billion, which admittedly is not chump change. The problem is how much capital they needed to secure that profit. Their financial assets as of year end totaled about $790 billion, so their rate of return on assets was less than 0.4%. In order to clear any profit, they had to borrow about $765 billion, and to borrow it at close to Treasury interest rates. Since Freddie Mac is an agency of the federal government, it enjoys a loan guarantee from the Treasury. Based on the guarantee, it IS the Treasury and it borrows at only slightly higher rates.[7] Suppose Freddie had to borrow from the

57

same trough as other corporations. Freddie has fantastically high leverage: $765 billion of debt on top of only $25 billion of equity, or about 31 times equity. Banks by contrast run debt (chiefly in the form of deposits and CDS) to equity of around nine times. Even if we let Freddie borrow at a spread of only 2.25% above Treasuries, their interest cost after tax would be about $10 billion higher. Without the subsidy from the U.S. Treasury, in 2005 they would not have made $2.9 billion; they would have lost $7.1 billion.

The moral of this story, other than the lesson it gives about gratitude, is to bring home in a particularly dramatic way the forces that prevail in our capital markets: in this case, the consumer lending market, and especially the home loan part of it. Home building and financing appear to be highly successful, growth businesses. Indeed, we seem to be on a path to pave over the states of Indiana and Illinois. But inside the house there is economic rot: the homes we build are not worth what it costs to build and finance them. We expected to find economic productivity, but all we found was uneconomic subsidies.

The example of NVR is broader than the homebuilding market, because their lack of profitability comes not so much from poor performance in the building business as from massive abuse of executive stock options. The abuse of options has been and continues to be systemic throughout corporate America. The regular poster boys of options abuse have come from the technology sector, firms like Intel and Dell Computer. The Congress pondered raising the bar, to rein in abuse of stock options, but lobbying by powerful business interests defeated that initiative. As a result, corporate America has continued to be a political slush fund, and this is certainly no less true of the building industry as it is of any other industry.

There is another, equally gripping example of political control over ostensibly *laissez-faire* markets, and that is the oil market.

The Politics of Oil and Gasoline

There are public markets in all the multitude of grades and sources of crude oil and in the various products made from crude oil, and especially gasoline. The markets, which function principally in New York and in Amsterdam, are the sites of trading in a large quantity of oil and gas. They are nonetheless the tail of the petroleum hound. The amount of product that changes hands in those places is dwarfed by the amount that is pumped and delivered under long term contracts between the major players—governments and private business—of the petroleum business. No government that controls large blocks of reserves, and even more so no private corporation that ships, refines, and retails oil products, would ever trust their fate to the vagaries of the public market. They need the security of long term agreements amongst themselves. All the same, the markets are lively and many smaller refiners and retailers use them to manage their supply needs. There are in addition many well capitalized speculators who are always on the look out for price anomalies. There are always enough small players in the petroleum business to bring prices back into line in the long run, so speculators can expect to make a living by finding the anomalies first.

The petroleum business is by nature a world of slow, almost glacial change. As Americans and Chinese people buy more automobiles, as the highways of Arabia are gradually extended, and as the oil production in America decreases toward zero, the price of oil and gasoline must drift higher unless new producing wells are tapped. If supply increases gain on consumption, the price will drift lower. The only pricing factors with the capacity to cause rapid price changes are exchange rates and the purchasing power of money, because the cost of crude oil and gasoline are real resource costs. The real price of crude oil was essentially unchanged from 1906 to 2001, although over the course of those eighty years there were many peaks and valleys. Left to itself, the petroleum industry would be a model of gradual change and smoothly evolving supply and demand.

Since oil is shipped a long way from the well to the refinery, and the refined products shipped further to the consumer, at any given time there is a lot of oil in the pipeline. In the United States, the pipeline contains about seventy days' supply, which is a little more than one billion barrels of oil. This quantity is not really a discretionary inventory because there is very little flexibility. The one billion barrels fill the existing facilities to the brim so there is little opportunity to store more, and on the other side, it is just enough to feed refineries and gas pumps, so there is little flexibility to draw it down. The only truly discretionary storage is the Strategic Petroleum Reserve, which is owned by the federal government. Its normal capacity at this time is 700 million barrels, but in an emergency the Department of Energy could sell it all. Other industrialized nations have their own strategic reserves too, though in practice the Japanese reserve is the only other one of quantitative significance. In the absence of war or natural disaster that closes the major shipping routes, the Strategic Reserve is the only reason for dramatic price changes. In other words, rapid price spikes—both higher spikes and lower spikes—are in practice always caused by decisions made in the Oval Office.[8]

To put it more directly, the Strategic Petroleum Reserve is a discretionary slush fund manipulated by the president of the United States, which affords him the power to move the price of oil a long distance in a very short time. The reserve is not large in relation to the oil business, so the effect is temporary, but very often the need is also temporary. Never has this capacity been so graphically demonstrated than in the run up to the mid-term elections of 2006. Earlier in the year the Reserve was a net buyer of oil, because its physical capacity had just been expanded, and so in early August oil ran to $78 per barrel. Over the next two months the Reserve was a net seller of oil—on the order of one million barrels per day—and the price conveniently collapsed to $58. Voters could hardly fail to notice that on the way to the polls they filled the tank with $2 gasoline! The shocking truth however was that this triumph seemingly changed few votes and the Democrats won the election. We can all commiserate with the president about the lack of gratitude shown by the American people.

What this example has in common with the other examples in this chapter is that it too shows how the fundamental economics of American business plans and markets are now displaced by political decisions from Washington. Long ago—or at least it seems long ago—American business and markets were the triumph of American thrift, ingenuity, and intelligence. Those were the days when American capital was the most productive in the world, and it carried the whole nation to the heights of wealth and power. Now by contrast American capital is the sick man of the world economy, surviving only on a steady diet of cheap credit and political largess.

Cheap capital never becomes healthy or productive or successful capital spontaneously. It is far more likely to become inefficient and failing industry.

Notes

1. Profits so far this year are falling off the pace of 2005, and are expected to total about $500 million for 2006, and significantly less than that in 2007.
2. November 14, 2006.
3. Actually, the management are also major shareholders, apart from their options. Clearly however they are in no great need of more cash, and prefer to defer their negligible dividends.
4. Wall Street brokers, who make a market in shares and who are paid for that service, will buy the shares if they expect to resell them at a still higher price. They are of course looking for profit on the trade, but they are not investors. Anyway, this news just in: as luck would have it, the shares of NVR rallied $50.50 today, to close at $584.5. At that price the outstanding options are worth, not $910 million, but a sumptuous $1,045 million. That is to say, another $135 million. The good news, or is it the even better news, is that instead of clearing $20 million over the last three years (2003–2005), NVR actually lost $115 million. As they say, "Easy come, easy go."
5. For reasons that are not entirely clear, the Treasury stopped issuing one year bills about ten years ago. It is however not difficult to impute a Year Bill from the panoply of other Treasury notes and bonds.
6. On an annual basis, that is a growth rate of 62% per year.
7. Freddie Mac pays about an added 1/4% above Treasury yields. That spread, applied to a debt of $765 billion, costs Freddie about a billion dollars after tax.
8. Not surprisingly, other major nations are getting into the strategic reserve business, especially China and India. Russia doesn't need a reserve because it is a huge producer, and Brazil burns primarily alcohol in its vehicles.

6

Subsidies As Far As the Eye Can See

The essence of free enterprise capitalism is to ensure that all economic decisions are based on the true costs of things. In the current jargon this is called price "transparency." If, to take a rather timely example, I want to drive the ultimate road hog, as long as the cost of fuel reflects its true cost I should be free to do so. No matter how high the price of gasoline and diesel, if I am willing to pay the price even if I get just one mile per gallon, that is my choice. I am not taking anything from anyone else. I am not using up "their" fuel. It's my fuel and I pay for it.

The essence of socialism is to hide the true cost of things, so that economic decisions are based on distorted prices and are therefore inherently foolish and wasteful. If the fuel for my hog really costs $4 a gallon, even though at the pump it costs only $2 per gallon, then I am being encouraged to waste fuel that other drivers need more than I do: fuel that is worth $4 to them and only $2 to me. The premise of socialism is that the citizens are not really capable adults, weighing choices and deciding accordingly. They are overgrown children who need to be manipulated and guided. They can't be allowed to cross the street on their own; they need some higher power to hold their hands.

The rationale for socialism is that there are things that "we" want the public to do, but that selfish calculations of cost and benefit would seemingly prevent them from doing. Leaving aside the question of why the "we" are so much wiser and more just and charitable than the "they" are, the error in socialism is that it fails to appreciate the true nature of rational calculations. In a previous chapter I used St. Francis of Assisi as an example of this. He was not poor because of an inability to do simple arithmetic. He didn't make that choice by mistake. He made that choice because he calculated that he could be much more productive if he stopped worrying about his personal income. His choice didn't make him less productive, it made him more productive. Francis would be very much opposed to the idea of manipulating economic relations in order to seduce people into following him for the wrong reasons. There will always be just enough Francis's if the people are left alone to make up their own minds.[1]

The United States and Western Europe today enjoy by far the most sumptuous standard of living that the world has ever known. We are enjoying first of all the fruits of centuries of technological innovation and resulting economic development. The tools that modern science and engineering have brought to the desk and the table are wondrous. We are also coasting on the broad world that the European explorers opened to their home countries, and eventually to everyone. The world of today, with expanding avenues of international cooperation, is the direct result of their larceny. These are the real foundation stones of our prosperity, but our standard of living exceeds even what these achievements have produced, because on top of them we bask in the comfort of the welfare state that brings them to us at deeply discounted cost. The rest of the world sees it, and the American people see it instinctively. The tide of immigration to Europe and America is drawn by the lifestyle of the welfare state. It is said that immigrants come here to work, and that is true but incomplete. They come here to work at the wildly inflated wages available in the welfare state. To put it more bluntly: we are all living on welfare. It is a given that our neighbors come here to live on welfare. We do.

When the welfare state started in earnest, in the 1930's, the cost of subsidizing everyone was borne by extortionate taxes paid by the rich, both directly in personal income taxes and extortionate inheritance taxes, and indirectly in the excessive taxation of the businesses and property that they own. But today, the rich no longer want to finance the welfare state; they too want to participate in it. It would seem that this should condemn welfare to a sure death, and in the end it probably will. In the meantime however our ability to borrow limitless money from the Developing World has defused the crisis. We have welfare for all Americans and Europeans simultaneously because we can borrow from Japan and China and OPEC to pay for it. The Democrats keep promising that they want to restore the older world order, where we soaked the American rich with high taxes and reserved the welfare benefits to the middle class, but of course this is only rhetoric. Democrats and Republicans both know very well that rich Americans vote, but Japanese citizens do not.

In this chapter I plan to look into some of the more transparent welfare subsidies, and then to conclude with a short discussion of where this ends up.

Prescription Drug Benefits

There have been many astonishing improvements in medicine over the last seventy years and more, and some of the most important of them are medicines: chemicals that change our body chemistry in beneficial ways.[2] But why do we subsidize the cost of them? If we subsidize medicines, why not food and clothing also? Since the clothes that keep us warm in the winter are at least as beneficial to you and me as medicines, why don't we also subsidize clothing?

The answer of course is that we the people like subsidies, and for some reason it seems more logical to subsidize medicines than parkas. So in every election the candidates vie heatedly for the honor of promising us "drug benefits" even more generous than the competition offers. I will not dwell on this topic because I think it speaks for itself. If medicines are more expensive than they need to be—if for some reason unnecessary costs are built into the selling prices—what we need to do is to find a way to correct that. But if the retail price of medicines is a reflection of their true cost, we need to accept paying for them. The alternative only promotes excessive dependence on medicines and underutilization of other forms of treatment. The subsidy does not buy better health; it only buys more loyal voters.

The cost of medicines has to be paid in one way or another. Subsidies don't actually make anything cheaper in reality. What do you and I give up in exchange for subsidized drugs? Where does the money come from? Does it come from training more and better nurses? Does it come from exercise programs that might prevent the medical crises in the first place? The money comes from something else, something that we should have more of. Perhaps a new St. Francis will be wise enough to tell us.

The Auto Industry

The American auto industry has been consistently unprofitable for decades. The situation has gotten out of hand, to the point where GM and Ford shares rally whenever they announce that in the latest quarter they did not lose as much money as had been feared. The problem is even more obvious in the fact that GM and Ford are it. There are no other American automakers, but Washington does not deem this to be a problem. In Washington it looks a lot more like the solution. The fewer cars we buy from Detroit, the more we buy from Japan. Japan lends the proceeds back to us. Life is, as they say, Gooood.

One embarrassment remains, and that is the discomfort of the employees of GM and Ford, who see their livelihood disappearing. So the automakers make regular trips to the Capital and the White House, seeking gifts of money to make it possible for them to continue to support the benefits their employees receive. Fortunately, Michigan is a large state and its needs can not be ignored. The pleas are heard and answered, and GM and Ford survive to lose money another day.

Agriculture

Subsidizing medicines for the elderly and keeping Detroit afloat with gifts of cash are not too expensive as these things go. The subsidies of American agriculture are far larger and more consequential. The study of agricultural economics, and especially the study of distortions caused by national policies, is an old and broad field in itself, and much too extensive for me to attempt to summarize here in any detail. Fortunately, a few readily available figures convey all that is necessary for our purposes.

The budget of the Department of Agriculture for year 2007 provides for total outlays of slightly more than $125 billion, which is about one per cent of GDP. Of that total, actual operations of the department take a relatively modest share. Most of the money goes either directly in supports to producers of food and timber, or to consumers in the form of food stamps. Specifically, subsidies to producers will total more than $57 billion.[3] Food stamps and related subsidies for the public amount to about $54 billion. So, more than $111 billion of the department's budget consists of transfer payments to farmers and to the public. To put that in perspective, it is on the order of 10% of all the money we spend on food.

The ramifications of these programs extend into many areas of national life. The most obvious, though also the most often ignored, is the impact on the nominal cost of food, and therefore in reported inflation. The part of the $57 billion which is paid to producers represents a very large share of their total income. Farmers and animal husbandry men plant more and pasture more in order to qualify for subsidies, and the retail selling price of food products is therefore depressed by the surplus, and by a large amount. The other part of that $57 billion is spent subsidizing exports, in order to deal with the surplus. When the average shopper goes to the supermarket, he or she is hardly aware that they have already paid part of the cost of their groceries. While the price tags in the market may seem pleasantly low, it is because they do not reflect the full cost of their food. Since the Bureau of Labor Statistics, which compiles the Consumer Price Index, looks only at the price of groceries, it finds that food is very inexpensive, and that there has been little price inflation. If they took account of the total cost of food, however, the picture would be much changed. Producer subsidies always cause the price of goods, and price inflation, to be understated.

There is a second ramification that clashes rather amusingly with some of the subsidies I discussed above. Subsidies to farmers to plant crops and to raise livestock obviously raise the value of agricultural land as long as it remains in agriculture. At the same time, we are subsidizing home building, which raises the price that developers are willing to pay for land to develop. Farmers, or at least owners of farmland, profit handsomely in the ensuing bidding war, but it is not clear whether we end up with more land in farms than we otherwise would, or if we end up with more, expensive housing developments. It is my unscientific impression that in recent years we have been hard at work paving over Indiana, and if that is correct, it seems that the developers are winning. The implication is that perhaps the Department of Agriculture has not been generous enough.

There is a third consequence that is actually far more significant than these two, although they are major distortions. That is the implications for international trade. We subsidize farming and animal husbandry. As a direct result, we are net exporters of food, to the disadvantage of farmers in places like India and Brazil. Instead of buying food from them, we are actually competing against them. Nowhere is this anomaly more evident—nowhere is it made more painfully evident—than when we sit down with them to negotiate the rules of world trade. To put the matter in a nutshell, they simply refuse to negotiate with us unless and until we are prepared to stop subsidizing our farmers to compete against them. The day may well come when trade matters are important enough to cause us to scale back the subsidies, but until then this conflict has prevented any kind of negotiation on trade matters with the Third World. The World Trade Organization regularly announces new rounds of trade talks, and sometimes they are actually convened, but shortly thereafter they are adjourned without result because of this impasse on agriculture.

The Tax Code and Distortions

The number of decisions that are now embedded in our national tax code, both for corporations and for individuals, is the stuff of legend. The tax rates and various tax exemptions intrude on the minutest choices that taxpayers make, favoring some activities like weatherproofing your house and purchasing a yacht, and disfavoring others.

These tax incentives have the effect of subsidies, and they are often described in those terms, but that is not exactly correct. High tax rates on some kinds of income are not "penalties," they are simply high taxes. Low rates applying to favored activities are not subsidies, they are simply low rates. We all accept that as citizens we have an obligation to pay our legitimate taxes, but that does not change the fact that until the I.R.S. sends their bill, all the money belonged to the taxpayer. For Uncle Sam to take less of your money is not a subsidy or a gift from him. It is lower taxes. Similarly, if he claims a larger share of certain kinds of income, that is not a penalty, it is just higher taxes. There are no "tax subsidies." It is our money, not theirs, and for them to leave a little more of it with us is not a subsidy. Nonetheless, the incentives and disincentives that litter the tax code do manipulate our decisions, to guide them to greater conformity with the will of the governors.

Conclusion

In this short chapter I have touched on several of the most noticeable and significant distortions that the federal government engineers. The net result has been to produce a true Welfare State: a state where all or nearly all the people are supported by some kind of subsidy which is designed, ultimately, to obscure the full cost of living and to engender a feeling of wealth and prosperity that exceeds even the abundance of this nation. We are all special interests.

The distortions produced by the welfare state however cause not only unjustified euphoria, but also unwise and wasteful decisions on our part. The welfare state will eventually impoverish us, not because it is somehow bad to feel good about our standard of living, but because we will undervalue the most valuable things we could be doing and to overvalue relatively unproductive activities. To be more precise, it is obvious that we have wildly excessive investment in homes, and have spread them out over far too much of the real estate. Yet at the same time, we have too great an investment in agriculture too. Worried citizens wonder why our industry seems to be—and is—dying. The answer is that industry does not thrive in a country that tries to become a suburb of itself.

Notes

1. The order of friars who flocked around St. Francis developed over time a kind of native communism, condemning property and wealth. St. Francis was unwilling to criticize them, but he made it very clear that he did not share their hostility to personal wealth and that his choice was based on what was best for him.
2. While pharmaceuticals get most of the credit for transforming medicine, developments in surgery and microsurgery are really more important because drugs rarely effect the kind of cure that surgery can. But the benefits of temporary administrations of chemicals to treat a wide range of crises in our health are undoubtedly a great boon to mankind in any case.
3. Source = Consolidated Budget of the United States, 2007; U.S. Department of Agriculture.

7

Where Are the Economic Assets of Tomorrow?

As we ponder the future and the challenges that lie ahead, we are naturally led to assess the great economic assets as they exist at this moment, and more speculatively to envision what will be the great assets in the future. There is certainly a large overlap, because intrinsic in the notion of an economic asset is durability. Great assets exert a kind of gravitational force on economic activity that persists for decades or even centuries. Nonetheless, the steady evolution of technology and of economic agents exerts a reciprocal force that diminishes existing assets and builds up new ones.

The kinds of economic assets that we need to fix on are quite specific things. It is true that the vast farmlands of the Amazon and of the central plains of North America are immensely valuable, and could be construed as "assets," but they are not assets as we want to use that term because they are not under the direction of any single controlling agent. Economic assets are managed assets, and not merely natural phenomena. I can give as working examples the list of what I consider to be the three most valuable economic assets today. First and foremost is the "Wintel" computer system; comprising both the Intel hardware and Windows software. Second is the Suez Canal, and third is the Trans-Siberian Railway. These do not derive their value from inherent characteristics, but from the connections they make with their economic environment, and specifically with the uses to which they are being put. The spectacular value of the Wintel system lies in the Internet, both for disseminating information and for effecting communication between nodes. Its value would be justified, moreover, by just the more mundane uses like word processing and data processing and for executing innumerable computer programs of mind-numbing complexity that are the foundation on which the connectivity rests. Like a common national language, the standardization implicit in Wintel computers facilitates communication between them, without in any way inhibiting the creative originally that comes from the human being that is using one of them.

There is a natural, inevitable progression by which what starts as an asset becomes a part of the economic environment. The Wintel system is undergoing that evolution at this time. It was initially the brainchild of a small group of entrepreneurs who had control of all its important features. At this time however there are competing operating systems that can run on Intel chipsets, and there are alternative chipsets that support Windows. The spreading of this technology and the loss of control by the originators is by no means a bad thing. The technology broadens and deepens and becomes accessible to more people, all of which is good. Nothing is lost in the process. What results in the end is however no longer an asset, because it is not manageable by any single decision maker. It will then be no longer an agent of change and of creativity. Others will create and will change things through it, by using it, but that computer system itself will cease to be the focus of change and creativity.[1]

74

Economies grow and become more productive by the creation of new assets and the flowering of their creative potential. Where are our new assets coming from? It would be easy to leap directly from this question to outpourings of alarm. Much too easy. American has an abundance of economic assets, as well as natural and manmade resources, practically unparalleled in the world. Just because it would not be listed in the same sentence with the Wintel computer architecture, an innovative new web site or storefront business is also a genuine and valuable asset. Yet it remains unmistakably true that American people—including this American person—are very anxious about how we as a nation are going to maintain our record of creating new assets. It is very unlikely that the next Wendy's outlet or the next apparel shop will address our anxiety in a material way.

Where are the new big assets to come from?

The federal government has always recognized its responsibility where innovation is concerned. The Wintel box is a very conscious result of research and engineering that was financed thirty to forty years ago by the Air Force. It was that subsidized research that produced the earliest integrated circuits made by Intel Corp. Operating systems for the early microcomputers sprang up more or less spontaneously as the need for them and the opportunity to use them first appeared. Long before the Internet, it was the opportunity to create packaged applications software—e.g. Microsoft Office—and to integrate across applications that drove the development of operating systems, and it was the shrewd and determined drive of one man, recognizing the synergistic potential of integrating all this software into one rather seamless product, to build Microsoft.

The Suez Canal and the Panama Canal, as well as the Trans-Siberian Railway, were undertaken under the direct sponsorship of various governments. The French and British governments ceded their shares in Suez and the United States later ceded its stake in the Panama Canal, but neither canal nor the railway would exist today without the initiative of political sponsorship. The *laisse-faire* tradition in economic thought has from the time of Adam Smith regretted or even positively denounced the partnership of political and business leadership and savvy. In that tradition, business is set in opposition to government and political and dynastic forces posed in opposition to private business. That is manifestly a false premise. There are farsighted and creative men and women in both the business community and in government who make vital contributions to the common cause of bringing great assets into being, for the benefit of the whole community and nation. It is very true, and many are the sad examples where this truth has been ignored, that governments cannot succeed alone in building or managing businesses, because for a business to succeed there must be clear authority at the top, and an equally clear commitment to economic efficiency. A business that limps along, losing money and probably alienating customers is a wasteful endeavor. Subsidies can not make it effective. They will make it even less effective than it was before. At the same time, business needs a very high degree of freedom of action, and that is rarely found in government operations. Government is very bad at running things because the authority to make changes and to enforce hard decisions is usually denied to the bureaucratic staff. We simply do not trust our rulers to have such broad discretion and such freedom of control, but these are completely essential to business: they are completely essential to the entity whose job it is to produce value from the assets they control. In brief, the role of government in the economy is essential, powerful, and at its best creative. The role of government is not, however, to manage operations or economic assets. It is almost always best—and indeed it is almost a truism—to privatize.

I have at times used a simple example to make this point. We take it for granted that local governments—with increasing intrusions by the federal government—should run our public schools, but that is by no means sensible. However, leaving this admittedly controversial proposition aside, we can I think easily agree on a more modest recommendation. The school system collectively owns tens of thousands of buildings, which it has to maintain, add to, remove, and clean. Why? Why should the school board be in the real estate management business? Sell the schools to people who do that for a living, and lease them back. If the real estate managers fail, move the school to better quarters where the hallways are clean and the blackboards are legible.

Where are the new big assets coming from, the ones that will serve the next generation and maintain American wealth and productivity? This is the very troubling question that a lot of Americans are asking. Some go so far as to ask if we are becoming another Third World country. More houses and strip malls, though they are assets, do not address this question. More troops fighting around the world don't answer it either, and in fact they bring it to the fore. Our armies don't even win us control of oil and other natural resources any more, as they did in centuries past. We are not creating significant new assets, and our government is incapable of changing that because its attention and its effort are directed to foreign wars.

We are not without innovations. Serious attention is at last being paid to alternative motor fuels from alcohol and from combustible trash, and in pharmaceuticals too there is rapid innovation. In the energy sphere, it is gratifying that nuclear power is back in play, but the status of our nuclear power industry today actually illustrates the problem. Because no new nuclear plant has been brought on line in more than twenty years—and that plant was designed about thirty years ago—our nuclear power technology is very outmoded. Washington has tried a couple of ingenious schemes for bringing us into the 21st century. One was to finance research on nuclear power, with the research being carried out jointly by us and Russia. Russian technology is far ahead of our own, and we hoped to learn from them. Understandably this innovation has succumbed to world political concerns. More recently, we have offered to finance nuclear development in India and to start them off with our rather archaic designs, in hopes that their scientists and engineers can bring them into the 21st century. At the moment it looks rather promising. The Indian administration finds this offer enticing, although it faces deep domestic opposition. Still, this scheme does not so much address our lack of investment in nuclear technology as it proclaims our deficiencies, and our neglect of this critical asset.

Besides the limitations of our nuclear technology, it turns out that we have even greater vulnerability in producing the enriched uranium fuel. We have only one enrichment facility still operating, and it supplies only a fraction of our current demand. Most fuel for our nuclear plants comes from Russia, so that in effect we will be selling enriched uranium fuel from Russia to India. Russia already sells fuel to India. What is our contribution? Apparently our contribution is the money. India has to pay full retail to Russia, but we are willing to absorb part of the cost, providing it to India at a discount.[2]

It is not surprising that our contribution is money. We are the money masters, the owners of Wall Street. We *do* money, but as time goes by we do less and less of everything else. Wall Street gets richer and richer with fatter bonuses every year while the rest of America borrows.

We need more, far more. The rest of the world is growing up around us, which is good in itself. It would be no credit to us to preserve our stature by keeping the rest of the world on their knees. The question of whether we are becoming a Third World country is not really germane at this time, but the anxiety that it expresses is very timely. A Third World country is a country that does other people's work for them. It is a country of foreign-owned assembly plants. It is a country of thin educational investment—plenty of schools of music but few schools of engineering, and it is a country where whatever engineers it does produce go off to find work in the first world. It is a country that is forced by necessity to live from day to day, selling its services each day to the people and the nations that own the vital assets.

About twenty years ago I attended a conference on finance and financial markets organized by my alma mater, the Graduate School of Business of the University of Chicago. On the panel were a collection of the most eminent financial theorists of the day, several of whom now sport very well-deserved Nobel laurels. At the time I was a lowly vice president of a Loop bank, though I was also the head of government trading at their investment subsidiary. Even though this conference followed closely on the crash of 1987, the mood was as ever upbeat. No cloud ever darkened the sky, in those days, over the University of Chicago school of finance theory. Markets were deemed to be efficient, *laissez-faire*—if allowed to work—ensured endless prosperity, and the Nobel committee was on the phone. The theory was compelling, but the reality would not consent. There really is, I insisted from my seat in the Nave, such a thing as Third World country. The difference between First and Third World is that in the Third World there are factories to assemble automobiles, but in the First World there are engineering centers to create and improve them. Economic agents—people and businesses principally—in the Third World Labor, but in the First World they Work.

Surveying the trends in many areas of business and economics, there appears to be insufficient attention at the state and federal level to those formative investments that become the roots of new critical assets. Washington especially has ignored domestic development, and has spent its capital enhancing international relations at the expense of our own economy. The formula is "Americans consume the fruits of other peoples' labor." Not for long; not for long.

A day of reckoning is coming because as a nation we have borrowed vast sums of money that needs to be repaid. How have we spent that cash? Will it produce a yield that will pay for itself and let us repay the debt? This is very doubtful. Great Britain is a chilling example, having borrowed even more heavily than we, and spent the proceeds on their own lifestyle. Now the debts are coming due and there is no yield, no profit to offset them. Britain must sell assets to repay debt, and even to simply pay interest on debt. Great Britain is today a third world nation, Minor Britain. Great Britain survives principally as a long running BBC serial. Like the Cheshire Cat, all that remains is the smile when the reality is gone.

Notes

1. Obviously, there is nothing to prevent a new asset—a new computer technology—from arising and ultimately replacing Wintel. I am not proposing that the digital computer revolution is over. I am only asserting more cautiously that the Wintel revolution is over.
2. We have many dealings with Russia that touch on vital needs. Russia is our source of Titanium, which is needed to make airplanes and missiles. Last summer we attempted to impose sanctions of the Russian company, Sukhoi, which makes jet fighters and sells them around the world. Unfortunately, Sukhoi is our source of titanium, so the sanctions would make it impossible for us to produce another airplane. Needless to say, the sanctions are gone and we are happy Sukhoi customers again.

8

Thoughts on Money Ssupply and Inflation: the Extra "S" Is for Extra Supply

Introductory Note

The essay that follows was written in the fall of 2004, about two years ago, for a conference that drew scholars from the whole Pacific rim. It represents an analysis integrating an expanded view of money and the macro economy applied to the American economy as it was then. I have not attempted to update the data or the conclusions, because the message of the essay has more to do with the method and concepts of the analysis than with the specifics of the world as it was in 2004. In place of updating the data in the essay, I have devoted the next chapter—More on the Money Supply—to a review of the subsequent two years, as a kind of scorecard on the predictions that I made in the original work.

Introduction

We have been peeking at the money supply statistics. Common sense warned us against such a risky venture, but curiosity carried the day, and so we peeked. Anyone would have done the same. It's like draw poker: you just have to see what you were dealt, even though you are resigned to that fact that you may regret it once you know.

The money supply has expanded in the last year at a rate not seen since the Second World War. The amount of monetary stimulus is extraordinary. Even more extraordinary however is the shocking absence of corresponding economic boom. The *stag* in Stagflation is already upon us, and the *flation* is here even if the Bureau of Labor Statistics can't seem to find it.[1] These are pretty strong claims. What is the evidence?

> *"Inflation is always a monetary phenomenon."*
> —Milton Friedman

When the money supply expands faster than the economy can absorb, prices and other costs rise. Always. The exact chain of events from cause to effect is not always the same of course. That leaves professional economists something to sharpen their pencils on, but Cause always has Effect. The first order of business at this moment is to review the evidence on the Cause: excessive monetary stimulus. This chapter combines three short pieces that explain this case. In this part I will fix on the Supply aspect: how do we measure the supply of money and, once we have settled on a measure, what has actually been happening to it. Then we can address the Effects.

The Money Supply

It is the unique privilege of central banks to supply money to their national markets. It is indeed a privilege, because the right to create money is the right to spend what was not earned. Central banks quite literally print new money and spend it. This, we can all agree, is not hard duty.

Historically, monetary economists focused narrowly on the money that a single central bank supplies to its own domestic economy, but the internationalization of financial markets necessitates our taking a somewhat broader view of the process. It is closer to the truth to say that central banks around the world combine to supply money to the world economy. But when we address money supply as it impacts our economy, or any single economy, we need to focus again on the amount of money that is being supplied to that economy. The new, more international perspective however reminds us that it is not only our central bank—the Federal Reserve Board—but the combined total of all central banks that are supplying us. We both make our own money and we import some more.

The story of how the Fed creates money should be pretty familiar stuff at this point. In brief the Fed prints money and uses it to buy bonds and notes of our federal government; government debt. The charter of the Fed actually authorizes the Board to buy anything. It is permitted to print money to buy your house, but in practice they have more self control than that. They limit themselves to government securities. That does not in any way however limit their effectiveness. The effectiveness of monetary policy derives from the fact that central banks create money—wealth, or at least the appearance of wealth—out of nothing and then spend it according to policy goals rather than profit goals. Central banks are in fact extremely profitable, for obvious reasons, but they do not let the pursuit of profits influence their decisions.

That is true of our Federal Reserve Board and it is equally true of other central banks. They—the foreign banks—also buy debt of our government and like the Fed they do not care about the investment merits of what they buy. When—to personalize the story—the prime minister of Japan gives the order to buy our bonds, the Bank of Japan buys. Period. End of story. Money that previously was not part of the wealth of America comes in to buy bonds, for reasons of policy unrelated to investment merit. The implication is that the true Monetary Base of this country is equal to all the bonds and notes that our Fed has bought *plus* government debt bought by foreign official organizations. By tradition, the term "Monetary Base" has been reserved for purchases by our Federal Reserve. The broader, truer measure therefore needs a new name: High Power Money.[2]

Recent History

With this preamble under our belts, we are inspired to look at what has been happening to High Power Money. The following chart puts this in perspective. The top line is High Power Money since the beginning of 1987. The lower line is the part which is the Monetary Base of our Federal Reserve; the gap is that part of the total contributed by foreign central banks.[3] Over that period of nearly eighteen years the Monetary Base has grown from about $250 billion to nearly $800 billion. The Fed has printed, net, about $550 billion and bought debts of our government with it. At the same time, the true High Power Money has expanded much faster, rising from $400 billion to about $2.2 trillion. Foreign holdings today are about ten times what they were at the start of this his-

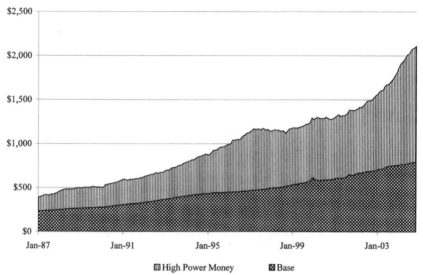

High Power Money
in $billion

Source: Monetary base: St. Louis Fed. Foreign official holdings on depostiy at the FRB: FRB.

tory. As a result, where the foreign contribution was only about 40% of the total in 1987, today it is about 65% and rising.

It cannot have escaped anyone's attention that the top line is climbing very steeply after early 2001. We need to take a closer look, and in particular we need to relate the rate of growth to historical reference points. Is the recent expansion of money just ordinary or is it exceptionally rapid or—for logical completeness—is it actually rather slow? I have already tipped our hand: it is astonishingly rapid. The particulars deserve a fuller airing. The graph below is based on the same data as the preceding chart, but we have converted it into annual growth

Growth Rate of High Power Money

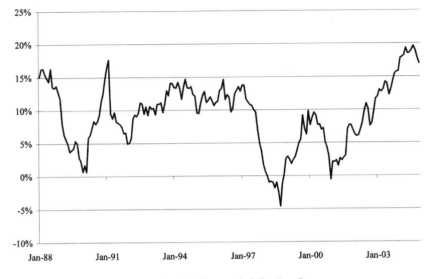

Source: Logistic Research & Trading Co.

rates. A word on the dating: we date the change over a year by the midpoint of the year, i.e. the percentage growth from April to the next April is assigned to the October between them. The most recent data therefore is dated March, 2004.

The first thing that leaps off the chart is the high variability of the growth rate of High Power Money. The range is from a low of minus six per cent to a high of around twenty per cent, and the turnaround from the lowest rate to the highest happened in only five years. At no time in recent history has the Federal Reserve been nearly as active. The spikes moreover correlate very highly with the business cycle. Starting with the unsustainable boom in 1987 that produced the crash in October

1987 to the credit crunch in 1989 that produced the recession of 1990/91, the growth rate of High Power money collapsed nearly to zero.

After a long period of stability lasting until early 1997, the growth rate absolutely plunged. This coincided with a mild recession at the end of 1998 and with the sudden rally of the dollar that bankrupted both Russia and the Asian Tigers. The rebound ran until early 2000, coinciding with the stock market bubble, followed by a crash until September, 2001, and finally a breathtaking bubble which continues to the present. For the period of about eighteen years, High Power Money has grown on average at a rate of little short of 10% per year.

What rate is normal and sustainable? We will have to return to this question in the next installment of this essay, because the answer has a lot to do with what we Americans do with our money: how we spend it. For the moment we can take a traditional benchmark which focuses on the domestic economy. There is no reason why the money supply would grow faster than nominal GDP. We hold money to spend it—it is the medium of exchange—and therefore how much money we want is roughly proportional to how much we spend. From this point of view, a growth rate of 10% is dangerous and a growth rate anywhere near 20% is explosive. There are fairly strict limits to how fast real output can expand. Nominal output—i.e. nominal GDP—can only grow faster to the extent that the price level is rising. The two sort of add up. If the money supply grows 20%, and if therefore nominal GDP also grows 20% but *real* GDP grows 3%, then the price level has to grow 17%. Per year! The actual rate of inflation can differ for reasons that are not directly related to High Power Money, so this is not an exact prediction. Nonetheless it is a force. Only extraordinary circumstances can hold the true rate of inflation much lower, and even those circumstances are temporary.

Whenever the money supply—High Power Money—is growing so much faster than real GDP can grow, that stage is set for very rapid inflation. There has never been an instance in American history when we avoided the inflationary consequences of such profligate money creation.

High Power Money and Its Components

I have made the case that the money supply is High Power Money, and that exactly where it comes from—whether from the Monetary Base of the Federal Reserve or from foreign official purchases of bonds and notes—does not matter. The effect is the same. The composition of the money supply does however matter when we set out to explain why it has grown so much. To address this question we have split out the two components and tracked them separately. The results are shown on the following chart. The chart actually tracks three rates of change: the money supply in total, and the two components. The path corresponding to the total supply is of course identical to the previous graph. We have included it to help put the two component parts into perspective.

The contrast between the Monetary Base and the Foreign component could hardly be starker. Apparent Fed policy has been consistently steady. The one exception to this generalization is that even Washington was caught up in the general euphoria surrounding the stock market bubble of 1999/2000. That episode shows up as a

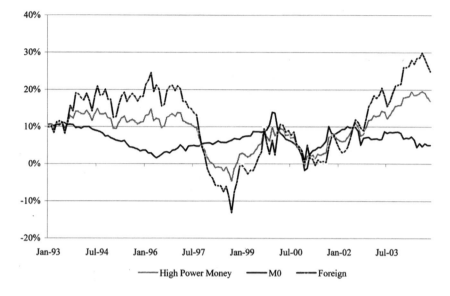

Source: Logistic Research & Trading Co.

spike in the growth rate of the Base in late 1998. The stage was then set for the bubble, and even the sharp tightening in 1999 was unable to stop it. Leaving this embarrassing indiscretion aside, the behavior of the Base over time certainly looks stable and consistent.

The Foreign Holdings component by contrast is right out of the wild West. Explosive growth follows dizzying plunges over and over again. My focus at this time is understandably on the most recent, explosive growth, because from a practical point of view, the present time is the only one that anyone can do anything about. History is indeed prologue, but it is still history. What we find historically is that the true money supply has been subjected to unprecedented shocks of rapid expansion and sudden collapse. Only during the gravy days of the mid-1990s was there relative stability in the money supply, and it has been the money supply that we import from abroad that has constituted the instability.

It is tempting to try to draw conclusions from the historical evidence, and true to form, we will dabble in rationalizing. Before I go further however I want to remind the reader that while data does not lie, neither does it speak for itself. The devil is not in the details, he is in our attempt to *interpret* the details. With that warning in hand, it seems that we can learn something from the data that sheds light on the thinking of the political and monetary leadership of the country.

The opportunity to manipulate the money supply by playing with the foreign component must seem almost too good to be true. To reheat the economy, demand of our worldwide partners that they pitch in. To cool an overheated stock market, lean on them to pull back. All the while, the Monetary Base executes tight, disciplined circles well calculated to convey the impression of calm and savvy monetary management. If there is any lesson that experience teaches, it is that when we mortals think we have a chance to have gain without pain, we cannot say *no*. When, in the case of the monetary managers, we can manipulate the money supply without appearing to, we go whole hog. Foreign holdings must seem like Chocolate Mousse light to Mr. Greenspan and to the White House. The problem is that there is no Chocolate Mousse Light and there is no way to grow the money supply explosively without causing an explosion.

Where Does It All Go?

Economists are a little different. They wonder where their money goes, just like everyone else, and they also wonder where *your* money goes. This is called looking at the Big Picture.

In the preceding sections of this chapter I talked about the money supply, pointing out that for the last few years it has expanded at an almost unprecedented rate and that a high rate of inflation is sure to result. The bridge from Cause—rapid growth of the money supply—to Effect—inflation—is not entirely simple or direct. The money that enters an economy flows—much like a river descending from the mountains—by way of several different paths. This section is devoted first to identifying those paths. The final part will take up the job of synthesizing theory and evidence to draw some conclusions about where we are going.

Where the Money Goes

There are only three things that can happen to a dollar that a household or a business receives. It can be spent, it can be paid out in taxes, or it can be put away in reserve to prepare for the future. Dollars received by governmental units have a simpler story; as everyone is well aware: they are always spent. Spending by governmental units does not however really enter this account, because nearly all of it is either expended on transfer payments—e.g. Social Security—or paid out in wages. These are important activities but they do not reflect the sort of decisions that need concern us here. It is only the public and businesses that make decisions that impact how new money is absorbed by the economy.

Taxes

While we are not concerned with how governmental units spend their receipts, the taxes they depend on are part of our story. Other things being equal, taxes absorb spending power of the public, and therefore they absorb money. Raising taxes is deflationary because it forces the public either to scale back purchases or to dip into savings. Tax increases have not however had a material impact on inflation or deflation in recent years. The Bush tax breaks are somewhat inflationary in theory, but in practice the overall tax levy from all governmental units has not diminished. On the contrary, it has grown somewhat.

The one area of tax increases that would be, and that may yet actually be, significant enough to impact inflation are property taxes. The revenue from property taxes has risen a lot in the last few years because the market value of real estate has risen so strongly. How much this has offset the inflationary effect of the supply of new money is an interesting but largely unexplored issue. It will remain so at least for the remainder of this chapter. We justify the decision to ignore the deflationary impact of the property tax on the grounds that the property tax has in any case not risen nearly as fast as the money supply. It simply cannot, therefore, explain more than a small part of how the new supply has been absorbed.

Saving

Money is not only the medium of exchange. It is wealth, and it is wealth of a particularly convenient kind. When we start to save, the first step is to let cash accumulate. Only when we have a bit set aside to carry us through financial rough waters do we begin to experiment with investments that have a longer horizon. As our capital grows, we take larger and larger chances, and the portion that we keep in cash shrinks. It simply is not as necessary to keep cash on hand because even in an emergency it would be possible to sell some investments to raise cash. The same process works in reverse. When the market value of investments falls, business and the public want to hold larger reserves of cash.

A stock market rally, in particular, lessens the demand for cash and a retreat increases it. Real estate values have in theory the same effect, but the demand for cash is not as responsive to real estate. The real estate rally in recent years provides homeowners with a cushion of wealth they can draw upon in an emergency, and so reduces the need for cash on hand. To the extent that the public can borrow against their real estate equity, it is a good substitute for cash, but few people would want to have to sell their homes. As a result, real estate is not nearly as good as substitute for cash as are stocks and bonds.

The chart below demonstrates that the consumer has not been on a borrowing binge in this decade.[4] Just the opposite. After the crash in 2000 the growth rate of debt balances has decelerated remarkably. The growth rate of credit card balances—called "revolving debt" on this chart—has fallen nearly to zero and stayed there for several years. Even non-revolving debt, which is predominantly mortgage debt, has decelerated. Consumer debt in

94

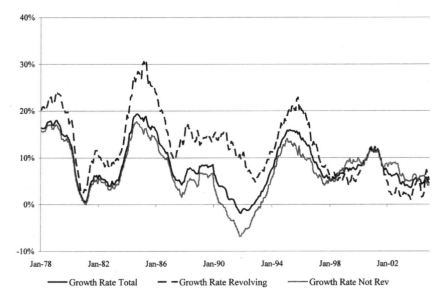

Source: Federal Reserve Board and Logistic Research & Trading Co.

total has grown at about the same rate as nominal GDP. It is very true that the American public is deep in debt. Decades of high rates of borrowing have left the public with a very large debt burden and the recent moderation has done little to address that condition. Nonetheless, it is very evident that the public is getting the message.[5]

American business is in very much the same situation as are households. We don't have a graphic to illustrate this point, but one single statistic conveys the reality just as well. Corporate America has accumulated aggregate cash balances of about $500 billion. That represents capital that has not been spent to build new factories or to rebuild existing ones. It is purely a risk reserve to ensure the survival of the businesses. Besides the usual roll-call of corporate America—the for-profit universe—there is a huge not-for-profit economy which has also been accumulating cash. Actually, not-for-profits have built cash balances at a faster rate than for-profit corporate America, because their non-profit status makes it impossible to return any excess to the investors.

Both the American consumer and American business—for-profit and not-for-profit—have gotten the message to build precautionary cash balance. The resulting accumulation of cash has absorbed a large amount of the supply of new cash. It also served to drive short term interest rates to an amazingly low level. Contrary to popular opinion, it was not the Federal Reserve that took short rates down to one per cent. It was the liquidation of investments—sales of stocks and bonds—and the accumulation of precautionary cash that lowered rates. The role of the Fed in such circumstances was merely to observe what was in progress and to ratify it with periodic announcements about Fed Funds. Lord Keynes had a term for this. He called it "pushing on a string:" a situation where increasing the supply of money does not stimulate investment and growth but merely responds to the public demand for the safety of cash.

The Trade Deficit

After paying taxes and accumulating cash, the other thing we do with money is to spend it. Since this chapter is devoted to money and inflation, the ultimate goal is to understand demand pressure on domestic prices. At the moment however we are simply doing an accounting of where the money goes and for that purpose it is essential

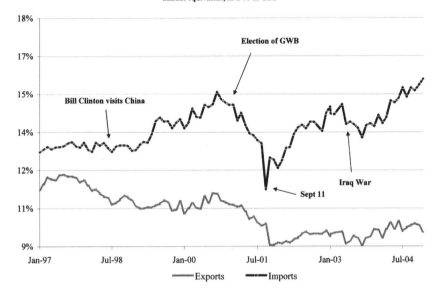

International Trade
annual equivalent, as a % of GDP

Source: Department of Commerce, Logistic Research & Trading Co.

to divide money that stays at home—money spent on goods and services made in America—from money that flies away—the trade deficit. Money spent to purchase imported goods actually leaves the country. It may come back soon, as investment or lending, but as money it does at least initially leave. For this reason, a trade deficit is inherently deflationary: it bleeds cash out of the economy.

It should hardly be necessary for us to document the astounding growth in imports and in the resulting trade deficit. This is one story that pops up regularly in the headlines, and always in unmistakably large print. Nonetheless it is worthwhile to devote a little space to what has happened in recent years. The chart above depicts im-

97

ports—the higher line—and exports as a fraction of GDP—the lower jagged line. It goes without saying that GDP has been growing, and since the deficit—the gap between the two lines—has been widening as a percentage of GDP, the deficit has expanded even more in actual dollars.

As of this moment the trade deficit is running at the rate of about 5.5% of GDP. In relation to High Power Money, the deficit each year is about one third of the entire High Power Money. The deflationary implications of a trade deficit are therefore of more than theoretical interest. This rate of losing High Power Money is more than merely bleeding, and approaches hemorrhaging.

Summary

The foregoing accounting is admittedly rather dry. It would be fair to say that if you noticed anyone around you that found it deeply engrossing, you can be sure that you are in the presence to deep and lasting commitment to economic theory. Dry but necessary. I will try to summarize here what it means in practice. In the last sections of this chapter I will endeavor to draw together all the pieces that I have talked about in the first and second part, to see what they say about where we are headed. We learned that the money supply has been "supplied" very, very generously since the crash of 2000. Actually, the high stimulus started earlier, in the financial crisis of 1998. It seems then something of a mystery why there has not been a surge in inflation as a result. Rest assured, the inflationary consequences are delayed, but only for so long. They are coming. But before we get to that part of the account, it is necessary to satisfy ourselves about why they have not been evident thus far.

The reason, of course, is that the trade deficit and the accumulation of precautionary cash balances have absorbed the lion's share of the new supply. Households, and even more so for-profit and not-for-profit businesses, have let their liquid cash build up without spending it or investing it. As Keynes dryly noted, expansion of the money supply has not been any more effective than pushing on a string.

The trade deficit has drained a lot of money out of our economy, and that is a nearly unique event in business cycle history. There is only one precedent for the massive injection of new money from abroad into our economy during a recession. Ordinarily in a recession it is up to the Fed to provide money, and they usually are slow to react. The demand for precautionary cash balances alone soaks up loose cash and the trade balance slips into surplus. The lone precedent for importing money from abroad is—interestingly enough and disturbingly enough—the Great Depression. In the early 1930's America ran a large trade deficit. It was precisely that deficit that motivated the Congress to pass the Smoot-Hawley punitive tariff bill. The rest is history.

On that note I will conclude this excursion into monetary theory. We will return to current events, focusing on where this is leading us.

Return of the Dollars

Is there any way, or at least any moderately plausible way, that America can avoid a rapid acceleration of the rate of inflation? No. There is one way on paper that it could be avoided, but there is broad agreement that we

All Civilian

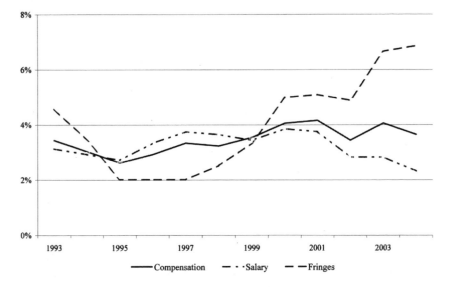

Source: Department of Labor, Logistic Research & Trading Co.

can not go that way. The way to avert the coming inflation would be massive, deflationary tax increases.

The preceding installment of this analysis, Part 2, dealt with the leakage which has quelled the normal inflationary pressure one would expect from highly stimulative monetary policy: tax increases, precautionary saving, and the trade deficit. These compete with domestic consumption. As a result, Gross Domestic Product grows more slowly than it otherwise would, and demand pressure on domestic prices is correspondingly less than it would otherwise be. But as they say, "What goes around comes around," or to put it differently, we can already see the headlight glinting on the tracks.

100

Present Inflation

It would be a mistake to think that inflation is not here already. We will detail in subsequent chapters the case that inflation statistics from the Bureau of Labor Statistics dramatically understate existing inflation. The B.L.S. data on employment costs however zero in on labor costs, which represent the lion's share of the cost of doing anything: not only business, but public enterprises and agencies are affected.

The preceding chart shows the year-to-year percentage change in employment costs over the last decade. Since the freshest data available is for the second quarter of 2004, the data point labeled "2004" actually covers the twelve months from the middle of 2003 to the middle of 2004. Previous years are similarly shifted. What the chart shows and places in historical context, is that over the latest two years—mid 2002 to mid 2004—fringe benefits have shot up about 14%. Total compensation is about 8% higher, but wages and salaries—spending money—have fallen behind inflation. The average employee is paid less in real terms, and has less purchasing power than he had in 2002, but he costs his employer more than he did then.

The stock explanation that is usually attached to these figures is that the same average employee is more productive today, and that his or her actual work costs the employer less, not more. That, at least, is the interpretation offered by the Chairman of the Federal Reserve. It does not stack up. First of all, if employees were becoming more productive, it would be their wages and salaries that would be rising. On the contrary, while wages are rising somewhat, they are falling behind inflation. Any employer, seeing that its workers had become more productive, would be willing to raise their wages and salaries. No employer would respond by offering to pay more for the same medical plan and to set aside more money to fund the same retirement benefits. The rapid escalation in outlays for fringe benefits does not reflect new-found generosity. It reflects that the benefits themselves have become much more expensive. By the same token, employees have become more expensive even though they have had to settle for very modest salary growth.

There is a second test which weighs in on whether it is productivity or cost inflation that has driven labor costs. The reason why employers raise their employees who become more productive is that the employer has become more profitable: worker productivity is highly profitable. This is not to say that employers would rush to raise their workers; they do it only because it is better than losing them. Everyone knows—and the stock markets know it best—that profitability in business America has been very poor for the last few years. Last year was a fairly good year, but only by contrast with the two years that preceded it. This year we're back to the bad old days. If American workers are more productive, why are their employers so unprofitable?

Many analysts including us have questioned the validity of published statistics that purport to show low inflation and growing productivity. Our essay entitled "The New Cross of Gold" summarizes some of this thinking and supplements the points I have just made about employment costs. We and many others are skeptical about the so-called "New Economy," and it is a valuable exercise to review those arguments. We do not however want them to obscure the main point of this essay, which is to peer into the future course of the cost of living.

102

The Dollars Return

A lot of dollars have found their way in the last seven years into precautionary savings of American business and households, and another lot of dollars have found their way into foreign hands as a result of the trade deficit. What would bring those dollars out of storage, and what would be the result if they do come out?

Let's start by tackling the first question, which asks what would free those saved dollars and put them back in circulation. The case of precautionary savings is unusual, because they will eventually be spent in any case: they will be spent whether they are needed or not. They are needed and will be drawn down if the threatening events actually take place. They are like insurance—actually self-insurance—and when they are needed they will be spent. This is not an entirely unlikely turn of events. Four years after the spectacular stock market crash, the market has not regained its lost ground, and the reason for that is that corporate profits have been deeply disappointing. Investors need their cash savings to make up for investment returns—dividends and capital gains—that have not materialized. Business needs the dip into the cash to support operations or internal investments that should have been financed from retained earnings.

The alternative is that the national economy emerges from the recession and investment gains flourish. In this case, precautionary savings will be spent because they are no longer needed. In fact, they are in readiness to finance the next boom when it comes.

The public is well aware of the high cost of precautionary savings, especially in an inflationary environment. They search for alternative investments that offer rates of return with some sort of inflation hedge, and real estate is the foremost of these. Accordingly, the public has spent lavishly on real estate and of course the abundance of money supply has made this much easier and more compelling. Real estate assets are not money; we do not mean to suggest that they be included in precautionary cash balances. The unique attribute of money is the security of its face value, and real estate values are anything but secure in that sense. Our point is, more simply, that the real estate bubble is a glaring example of the broader desire of the public to "Do Something" with all that expensive cash, and especially to do something that will serve them well if and when inflation returns. The real estate boom has added risky real estate values to relatively safe cash balances in the public capital account. What it has not done is to change the logic of precautionary savings: they are going to be spent whether they turn out to have been needed or not.

The situation with foreign holdings of dollars is somewhat different, because their motive for accumulating dollar balances is very different. As long as there is net foreign demand for dollars, the trade deficit can continue to run and it seems that the dollars will never come home. The climate for dollar holdings—as an asset—has become and continues to become more threatened and much less likely to persist. Equally worrisome are the consequences of the trade deficit on our domestic, American economy. The results of years of cumulative dollar outflows will be much the same in the coming years as they were in the 1970s, and for the same reasons.

Stagflation is the term coined thirty-some years ago to describe a period of simultaneous inflation and slow real growth. The orthodoxy of Keynesian economic theory supposed that such a combination would be impossible, but the new monetarism of Milton Friedman demolished the theoretical pretension of that belief at the same time that current events trampled its empirical plausibility. Rarely in history has a scientific controversy been decided in such a dramatic and costly fashion. Stagflation is the fate of any nation in times when its currency is falling in value faster than it can redress a structural trade deficit. Since it takes years or decades to redress a structural trade deficit, the only unknown in the time dimension is how fast the dollars want to come home.[6] Hence our focus on the "Return of the Dollars."

It will come as no surprise to anyone who has followed our analysis this far that we are anticipating another chart, and of course he would be right. This one has to do with the exchange value of the dollar: how much of foreign currencies a dollar will buy. There are many foreign currencies with interesting stories to tell, but for our purposes the most revealing exchange value is the one that exists between the American dollar, on the one hand, and a basket of all foreign currencies. The Federal Reserve Board tracks precisely that sort of basket. It is a basket of foreign currencies bundled into standard units: A Unit of the basket consists of a specified number of Yen, some number of Euros, another number of Canadian Dollars, and so on. The Value of our Dollar is simply how many of these units a Dollar will buy. This value has been dubbed the "World Value of the Dollar" by the Fed. The following chart depicts the recent history of this series.

Starting in May, 1995, the dollar rose fairly steadily for six and a half years, until the end of January, 2002. With remarkable swiftness the trend reversed, and the declining trend continues to the present time. Along the way there have been limited departures from the trend. The most obvious of them is the chaotic dollar rally in 1998 associated with the collapse of the Russian economy and coincidentally with the strengthening of commercial

FRB Broad Dollar Index

Jan 30, '02

Source: Federal Reserve Board, Logistic Research & Trading Co.

ties between China and America (President Clinton visited China in the summer of 1998 which led to China's accession to the W.T.O.).

The event that preceded and caused the sudden reversal of trend was the sudden surge in our imports that began in September, 2001. We have presented the time series chart of the trade deficit already and need not repeat it here. From the election of President Bush in 2000 until September, 2001, the trade deficit was being addressed, and imports, in particular, were shrinking rapidly. All of that changed after the felling of the World Trade Center, and the deficit has subsequently grown explosively. I can only speculate why the balance of trade would coincide with the War on Terror. It is very evident that America obtains a lot of influence over the policies of other nations by the simple expedient of buying everything they want to sell us and not asking them to reciprocate by buying from us. We have written at some length elsewhere about this dynamic.

If it was a decision of the federal government that prompted the huge deficits, it was a terribly short-sighted decision. The world simply does not have a limitless demand for the dollars that pile up in their bank accounts as a result. Currency traders even anticipated the imbalance, and the dollar had started to fall even before the deficits had become completely unsustainable. Unfortunately, the correction that has been in progress for about twenty months has a built-in accelerator. The foreign public is frankly much more willing to hold onto their dollars when the dollar is rising in value. When the simple glut of dollars, accumulating from the current trade deficit, begins to weigh on the value of the dollar, there is by that time an ample supply of old dollars and they are getting increasingly nervous.[7] What happens when dollars come back from off shore?

They are used to buying things. To the extent that they buy goods and services, they raise prices of things and cause price inflation. It is an empirical question how fast real output can expand to meet export demand, but the scale of the dollar imbalance at this time is a guarantee that the inflationary consequences will be large. The things that we can quickly do more of—the auto industry for instance—are the ones subjected to the most intense foreign competition. It seems unlikely in the extreme that Japanese and German drivers will be ordering their cars from Detroit. Bulk commodities are equally unpromising. The most valuable one is of course crude oil. Our domestic production is however tending down, and in any case supply is not highly price elastic in the short run. Food grains we have in abundance, along with other, higher-valued crops—but they are not valuable enough to absorb many dollars unless the prices rise astronomically. There are only two crops—corn and soy beans—for which the total value of the annual crop is more than a relatively few billion dollars. Pharmaceuticals could be a promising area to expand exports. Our trade surplus in them is already large. The problem with this solution is that all around the globe, medicines are purchased not by the sick but by their governments: more specifically, their public health services. They are not going to purchase a lot more drugs unless they plan to treat a lot more people. Summing up, year after year, while our imports have grown explosively, our exports have remained almost constant in relation to national GDP. The items that we could plausibly export a lot more of simply do not seem to be things that the world wants to buy a lot more of.

The other route that repatriating dollars can take is that they can be spent to purchase assets: stocks, bonds, real estate, and the like. It is highly unlikely that they will go into the stock market or bonds because the threat of inflation makes these kinds of assets very unpalatable. Not only are foreign investors much more likely to be selling stocks than buying them, they will be competing with domestic investors to get their sales off. Real estate is more promising, but the result of squeezing so many dollars through such a narrow window would be a real estate bubble of frightening proportions. In any case, asset sales are not production. The American who sells real estate is no more likely to want to hold the dollars he receives than was the foreign entity that brought it, and whoever eventually spends the dollars on goods and services is adding to nominal final demand and to price inflation.

The dollars that are now coming back into our economy have to ignite inflation. As I mentioned above, moreover, this process contains an automatic accelerator.

Inflation is the great score keeper, reconciling how rich we think we are with what we are actually able to afford.

The Value of a Dollar

One inevitable byproduct of repatriating of dollars from abroad is that the purchasing power of a dollar falls. Most of this depreciation is still in the future, but there is one item of trade that is forward looking: gold. Even more so, it is a store of value which mirrors expectations of future inflation. Except for brief explosions of discovery of new mines, gold is a reliable standard of real value because it is highly durable—it's physical properties do not change with time—and because the cost of extracting each ounce of metal from the ground is pretty constant over time. The recent history of gold is therefore a valuable measure of the real value of the dollar. The following chart takes us from the mid-1990's to the present.

The valley that so clearly defines this history is a signal of forces of disinflation that were so characteristic of the 1990's. Our previous charts failed to focus as clearly on that phenomenon. The last decade started with an unsustainable peak which was left over from the very aggressive monetary policy that pulled America out of the recession of 1991, and earlier from the depression of 1980–82. Aggressive money creation had rattled the markets' confidence in Mr. Greenspan's commitment to inflation fighting. On the eve of the crash of 1987, gold hit

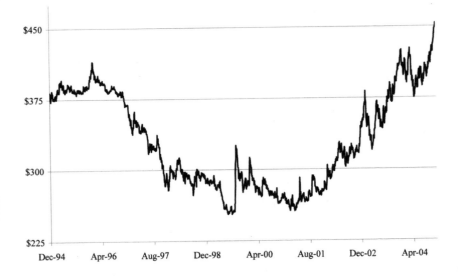

Price of GOLD, in Dollars

Source: Logistic Research & Trading Co.

$500. The trough reached in the late 90's was the tag end of the long decline from that panicky level. The collapse of the Russian ruble and simultaneously the panic in the Asian currencies signaled that indeed we had won the Cold War, and we were expected to define the new world order. The long disinflationary trend of the preceding two decades was at last confirmed, ushering in the epoch of the strong dollar, the heyday of the Federal Reserve and of its tight-money chairman. As so often happens, this trend was reversed at just the time that it was finally accepted as an established fact.

The consequences for the rest of the world were not entirely pleasant. With the exception of China, every other nation that tried to tie its currency to ours suffered through very agonizing deflation. Argentina, Thailand, the Philippines, and above all Russia were driven into bankruptcy by adopting a currency that they could not afford. We however prospered as we had never done since before the Crash of 1929. This period was in every way a legitimate heir of the Roaring 20's.

The gold market never takes life easy, and the bottom of the market—roughly covering the three years from the end of 1997 to the end of 2000—was no exception. Starting from that time however the rally has been pretty consistent—about as consistent as this market ever gets—and has brought us at this point to a price level that we had not witnessed since the crash of 1987.

The ramp that we could confidently date from 30 March 2001, coincides with the explosive growth of the trade deficit, the equally explosive growth of the fiscal deficit, and the expansion of high power money: in other words, the three fundamental realities that have occupied this essay. There is therefore no need to belabor the point any further. The stage has been set for a return of very serious inflation and a dramatic decline in the exchange value of the dollar.

Notes

1. The term "stagflation," coined in the 1970s, is the merger of stagnation and inflation.
2. This is not a new term. It has long been used by economists as a synonym for Monetary Base.
3. Actually, a small part of this comes not from central banks, but from international organizations like the IMF and the World Bank. They represent however only a very small component.
4. The raw data for this chart comes from the Federal Reserve Board. Actual preparation was done by Logistic Research & Trading Co.
5. The problem of household debt is principally one of distribution. The

rich always save and the poor always borrow as much as possible. As the gap between rich and poor in American has expanded, so too has the debt problem of the working poor.

6. It is not strictly necessary for the dollars to have actually gone anywhere in a geographical sense. Dollar balances held in New York or Chicago, but owned by a foreign entity which would rather keep them as an asset than spend them, are dollars that have found a home with someone who sells things in America, and that as a result have been removed from circulation here.

7. It has been documented repeatedly that foreign exchange is not an "efficient" market. After the fact it exhibits runs that a smart trader could exploit for profit. This inefficiency persists because in the foreign exchange market, as in so many markets, conditional equilibrium values are path dependent, but the paths are not paths of efficient prices. Therefore, equilibrium is not an efficient price. In consequence the actual prices—which are trying to settle in on the conditional equilibria—can not be efficient either. This reasoning appears to be circular because it is *possible* for foreign exchange to be priced efficiently. Efficient pricing is a logical possibility, but it is unlikely. Inefficiency is both a more likely and a more stable state, as empirical research on exchange rate histories has documented.

9

More on Money Supply:
The Last Two Years

The preceding remarks were the state of our art as of autumn 2004, but life goes on. Two years later, in December 2006, the dynamics of money supply and prices have evolved in ways that should perhaps have been predictable. The consequences however of other, external events along with the consequences of Fed policy of the intervening 24 months have moved the economy to a very different situation.

The inflation that we predicted—contrary to the prevailing consensus of the time—has emerged clearly. I will not take time here for self-congratulations. There is always time to party, but at the moment there is a brooding presence which demands our full attention. The dollar has come face-to-face with the reality that it has been overvalued for a long time. Dollar strength has been the little engine that could pull us around Mr. Greenspan's Virtuous Cycle. The descent of dollar weakness therefore signals backsliding and trouble. The way down is not however an exact repetition of the ascent. In this chapter I will consider this final chapter of the story of dollars and inflation in the first decade of the new millennium.

World Liquidity Out of Control

The world money supply has grown at an unsustainable pace for much of the last decade. Japanese interest rates were held to a quarter of a percent for that entire decade, though the natural inflationary consequences were offset by accumulation of Yen in neighboring Asian countries. China's money growth is as impressive, but can be justified by the rapid monetization of their economy. India and Russia have been playing in the same band. In the case of Russia, aggressive money supply is to a large degree forced on them by sales of oil and gas. Since they receive dollars for the fuels they export, the selling entity—whether private or public—finds itself with growing dollar holdings. They in turn go to their central bank to exchange dollars for money—Russian rubles—which forces the bank to print more rubles. India's case is more similar to China. The explosive growth of monetized transactions—transactions in Indian Rupees—forces the Bank of India to accommodate. Where will it all end?

There must surely be congenital optimists at large, whose reply is that it doesn't ever need to end. More experienced hands, by contrast, know this process and know also that it always ends. In the recent decade we hear echoes of the 1920's. During both epochs world industry developed and grew at an unsustainable, indeed euphoric, pace. It began in 1920 with the end of the War To End All Wars. In 1995 it was the end of the Cold War. More important than these political transformations, the transformation of industrial and transportation technology and its transmission around the globe opened opportunities on a mind-boggling scale. It is an old proverb that nothing succeeds like excess. For the 1920's and its aftermath, no illustration could be more compelling than Argentina. We do not yet see which recent success stories will leave the most painful hangovers, but it is a proverb that is not to be dismissed without cost.

It would be a useful and instructive exercise to wade through world data on liquidity, but it is not necessary for our purposes because there is a single comprehensive measure of excess liquidity: the rising price of gold in relation to the average of world currencies. There is no single aggregate measure of the value of world currencies, but the Federal Reserve produces a fairly good proxy, named the "World Dollar Index." By its construction, it leaves out the American dollar itself—it is a value index of all other world currencies in relation to the U.S. dollar—but it permits us to reduce a vast number of time series—one for each currency—down to two: the dollar and the world dollar.[1] The following chart traces the history of the dollar, the world dollar, and the yen in one very revealing dimension: How much gold a constant amount of currency would buy. In the case of the dollar, it is how much gold $1000 would buy. For yen, it is the gold value of ¥100,000; and for the world dollar, it is the gold value of 1000 world dollars.

Almost every national currency has slipped in value relative to gold. The reason is not by any means that gold has become scarcer. Quite the contrary. These years are close to the all time peak of mine production of gold. Not since the high tides of the Yukon gold rush and the South African gold rush have mine production exceeded our production today. It follows rather obviously that if gold is not becoming scarcer, national fiat currencies must be getting less scarce—a *lot* less scarce.

For the gold value of world currencies to fall 50% in six years—a rate of about 12% per year—points to a very high rate of liquidity creation and a very high rate of

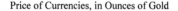

Price of Currencies, in Ounces of Gold

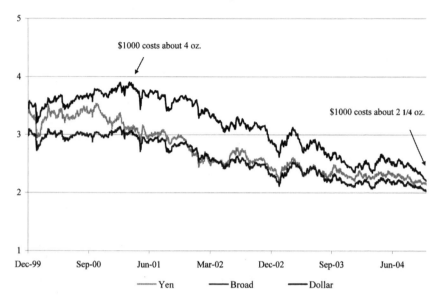

$1000 costs about 4 oz.

$1000 costs about 2 1/4 oz.

——— Yen ——— Broad ——— Dollar

Source: Logistic Research & Trading Co.

worldwide inflation. If gold had simply held a constant real value, we would have 12% inflation. The high rate of mine production has certainly served to depress the real value of gold, as has the net selling of gold reserves by European Treasuries. Nonetheless, it is possible that gold has actually grown in real value—a point I will return to shortly—and to that extent the actual rate of inflation in terms of national currencies would be less. As far as the rate of money creation however, that must actually have exceeded 12% per year because the world economy has grown in real terms. It is a simple accounting identity that the money supply growth can be sorted into the sum of growth of real economic activity and excess liquidity. If real growth has averaged 8%, total money supply should have expanded at the rate of 8%, plus 12% and then minus {growth rate of the real value of gold}. The answer is not obvious at the moment, but one would expect the true number to fall somewhere in the range from 15% to 20%. The true rate is much more likely, moreover, to have been higher than lower than this estimate.

A closer look at the chart reveals a second fact that should be very surprising. On average, while all these currencies have been highly correlated, the biggest drop has been the dollar. The U.S. dollar used to lie significantly higher than the others, but now all three are nearly together, which means that the value of a dollar has fallen more than the others. In the preceding chapter I separated two terms that are usually synonyms: High Power Money and the Monetary Base. The Base is the money created by the Federal Reserve Board; that is the usual understanding of the term. High Power Money however I equated to the Base plus dollars injected into the American economy by foreign central banks. There has been a sharp divergence between the two in the past decade, with the Base growing timidly while foreign central banks have showered recycled dollars on us. This divergence is hardly surprising; it is the manifestation of the Greenspan policy of the strong dollar. Keep Dollars scarce, but let dollar demand for government debt run wild. That combination of events works wonders as long as the dollar is actually rising, because foreign lenders want to keep their financial assets denominated in dollars. When they buy Treasury notes, they earn both the stated yield and the appreciation of the unit of account.

When the dollar starts to slide, under the growing weight of the trade deficit, the logic is reversed. Bonds and notes denominated in dollars are no longer very profitable assets to hold, interest rates rise, and the dollar starts to decline.

Deflationary Inflation

Inflation always gives way to deflation. The reason is very easy to explain. Inflation is the result of a collective illusion: the collective overestimation of wealth. Now look how this applies to credit cards. Thanks to the largess of foreign lenders—not only their central bankers, but all their financial institutions as well—banks that service credit cards are advertising on the television to put their card in your wallet, and lest you be unmoved they are calling you regularly to sharpen the message and make it more personal. In a world without inflation, you would have become a candidate for that card if your ability to use it wisely had improved. In that world, the flattering appeals would send a very sensible message, that you are more creditworthy than you were before. In an inflating world—a world of excess liquidity—the truth is that lenders need you more than you need them. The symptoms however are quite identical. Their TV adverts are just as witty, if not more so, and their phone calls just as frequent and heartfelt, if not more so. They are telling you that your credit has improved, where in fact it is their credit that has fallen. Everyone who experiences these appeals is being told that he is now richer, but he is not, in the measure of the gap between nominal dollars and actual wealth.

Inflation is the corrective: the path by which unrealistic expectations are confronted with reality. But it is not the end result. It concludes with the recognition of real wealth, and with a trail of disappointments and broken business and financial commitments. But they strew deflation wherever they are found, not inflation: real wealth destroyed as collateral damage from the collapse of unrealistic expectations.

The Dollar Exchange Value Revisited

I noted about the fact that amongst the world's currencies, the U.S. dollar has declined faster than the average currency. What is so remarkable is that throughout the decline the Federal Reserve Board has maintained a strong dollar policy. Arguably, without the strong dollar policy, the dollar would have slid faster, but the policy has manifestly not been successful.

There are two parts to a strong dollar policy: the domestic money supply must be held in check, and some key foreign money supplies must grow rapidly, and a large part of that liquidity from abroad must find its way into our economy. I documented both of these practices in the preceding chapter on money supply. The Monetary Base of the United States—money created by our Federal Reserve—has grown slowly and in a very disciplined way while High Power Money has grown explosively. Restrictive domestic monetary policy by itself would result in a strong dollar, but only at the expense of high real interest rates and economic stagnation. When foreign central banks are willing to provide liquidity by accumulating our government debt, the financial markets are flooded with cash, interest rates are low—or at least not high—but the actual money in circulation—crisp new tens and twenties—expands slowly. They retain their scarcity value.

The result is almost indistinguishable from the Best

of All Possible Worlds.[2] The national currency itself becomes the defining component of the national wealth, as though money was in any way real wealth at all. The Wealth of Nations is spread out before us, and we take our pick of it because we have dollars to spend. As for who it is that is providing liquidity to our economy, the list is long. Two Asian powers however vie for pride of place: China and Japan. Japan alone has lent nearly ¥200 trillion around the world in the last ten years, and as a result their domestic money supply—yen issued by the Bank of Japan—is today actually larger than ours![3] The ratio of American money in circulation—an aggregate that includes bank accounts, money market balances, bonds, and a host of new financial innovations all denominated in dollars—and the Monetary Base is called the Money Multiplier. One sure mark of the Best of all Possible Worlds is a shocking rise in the money multiplier. Actual yen (Japan) and actual yuan (China) are transmuted through the magic of financial engineering into ersatz dollars.

The world needs monetary reserves. At any given time the list of truly creditworthy sources of liquidity is never very large, and any institutions that have that credibility are generously rewarded. They are able to count their money as wealth, because they can spend it freely. Other nations are only too happy to acquire dollars in exchange for real goods. The resulting trade deficit initiates a kind of virtuous cycle, in which our domestic money supply contracts because dollars are leaving the country to be salted away overseas. Other things being equal, the dollar appreciates because fewer are circulating. The dollar rises in value, and its status as the reserve currency is strengthened. Reserve currency status is by its nature a self-reinforcing condition. All that is required is for the central bank—our Federal Reserve Board—to exercise enough self-discipline to preserve the aura of reserve value for the money. As external dollar balances expand, the foreign institutions that own these reserves become moreover active defenders of their reserves. They have a powerful financial incentive to stop any run on the dollar, because for them dollars are a key part of their national wealth.

It is against this backdrop that we return to the weakening dollar. Despite very tight money, prices of internationally traded commodities have been rising methodically for years. While gold is, strictly speaking, a commodity, we do not want to focus on its value in this context. Gold is for these purposes reserve money. The commodities we need to track are those homely products like aluminum and steel, crude oil and natural gas, zinc, soy beans and corn, Portland cement, electricity, and rubber, that are brought and sold, and therefore priced, as reasonably homogeneous aggregates.[4] Among these, crude oil attracts the most attention today.

The Economics and Politics of Crude Oil

There is a lot of petroleum in the world. The magnitude of the recoverable reserve is not known, because vast amounts of it are found in environments that are not economically feasible today but that could be exploited whenever they are needed. Several individual pools—the Athabasca tar sands in Canada, the heavy oil reserves in Venezuela, and the oil shale fields in our Rocky Mountains—each encompass more petroleum than all of the Persian Gulf nations did when we began to extract their oil. Before these sources became economic, it would probably be cheaper to use liquid fuel from renewable sources, especially alcohols, but the world is richly endowed with liquid fuels and with the carbon they are made from. "Scarcity," understanding that term as a kind of physical constraint, is ever-present, but it is by no means an absolute. Everything can be had for a price.

The world today is fixated on the shocking rise in the price of crude oil, and it is perhaps natural to think that it is caused by greater real scarcity, but that is by no means true. The shock wave passing through the petroleum market today is exaggerated by the panicky reaction of consumers who want to insure their own stocks by building reserves of oil and gasoline. A shock is therefore a self-reinforcing phenomenon for a period of time, and in that sense it is possible for petroleum to become temporarily scarcer in its true, economic sense of scarcity.[5] But as we use the term "scarcity" in everyday conversation, we really mean not scarcity, but worsening scarcity. What is going on today in the petroleum market is not an indication of worsening scarcity.

If petroleum was becoming scarcer, it would be wise to invest in alternatives. We as a nation have spent the last sixty years or more promoting the automobile. It is woven through our way of life. Shopping malls with spacious parking. Distant bedroom suburbs, and plotted housing developments growing out into rural countryside. Boss cars. Hummers and pickup trucks. And the list does not stop there. Riding mowers and weed whackers too. Chain saws. Cities dissolving and becoming suburbs of themselves. It would be hard to imagine how we could possibly consume more petroleum each day. There is nothing wrong with that. The ways we use oil are good in themselves, though they must compete with other goods that we have given up. The right response to growing scarcity would be to change that way of life in important ways, or at least to make it available to a much smaller slice of the population. Some of these changes will occur, though not because of the cost of gasoline. Agricultural commodities are also becoming more expensive because of the loss of farmland, and that had better stop, before we have to import corn and soy beans too. Even as petroleum becomes more expensive, however, the alternatives also rise in price, and that is not scarcity, it is inflation.

As crude oil rises in price, it is not the real cost of fuel that is rising—the real scarcity of oil that is worsening—but the real value of dollars that is falling. One simple chart drives this fact home. *The Journal of Commerce* tracks the prices of many commodities and combines them into a single index. Food stuffs like wheat and corn are not included, because the index is intended to correlate with the cost of raw materials purchased by manufacturing.[6] Petroleum and natural gas are certainly included in the index, but they are a much smaller share than one would naively assume because most of these fuels are consumed directly by the public. The total share of all fuels—oil, gas, and coal—used in industry is not much more than half as large as the weight given to metals, because bulk metals are exclusively industrials raw material. The chart below shows about ten years of history of the index compiled by the *Journal of Commerce*. This index trended steadily down through the 1990's, as the fruit of globalization. The embracing of Russia and the other pieces of the former Soviet Union was a particularly significant event for this purpose, because Russia is such a large source of metals. The growth of the Chinese steel industry was also very important. As of today, China is the leading producer of steel. Petroleum experienced a simi-

Journal of Commerce Price Index

Source: Journal of Commerce and Logistic Research & Trading Co.

lar decline, and by the end of the decade domestic crude oil was selling under $12 per barrel.

Not all commodities have risen in price, and petroleum has risen the most by far. West Texas Intermediate Crude bottomed in 1999 at under $12 per barrel, and peaked recently at about $75. Nonetheless, the most important lesson to derive is that commodities on the whole have rallied in dollars. It is not just energy.

Much of the rest of the world is populated by developing economies that depend critically on sales of relatively simple, "raw" materials. Actually, undeveloped or developing economies are characterized by a comparatively low level of human capital in the labor force. Their labor is devoted principally to relatively routine jobs like min-ing and drilling, farming and forestry, and the like: activities that have been practiced for many centuries. The contribution of human knowledge and skills to the value of the product is relatively small, as compared with computer design and biotech engineering, and the contribution of natural endowments—sun and soil, reserves of ore, open land, and so on—are correspondingly large. This state of affairs is actually synonymous with a low stage of economic development. As a nation begins to develop it is only natural that its first moves are to produce more of the traditional commodities, because its productivity in those fields initially grows faster than its development in most highly technical and engineered industries. It is almost always the case that economic development begins with rapidly expanding population, which is fertile ground for simply doing more of the tasks that were already being done. Later, as Adam Smith observed in his famous law that states "The specialization of labor is limited to the extent of the market," the deepening of traditional industries creates markets for specialized technological skills and products, which readily appear on demand.

The revolution that goes by the name of "globalization" coincided with a dramatic increase in the production capabilities amongst the developing countries. There are more significant oil and gas producers than ever before, touching every continent. The green revolution has opened a cornucopia of agricultural output and marine farming has for the first time made fish and other sea foods dietary staples around the world. Driving these developments has been a significant deepening of the world's population. In sparsely settled regions productivity is necessarily low. This is of course the downside of Smith's law of specialization. Poverty, caused by low productivity, has compounded low population density particularly in tropical areas, stifling precisely the gains in population density that are needed to raise productivity. Thus backwardness, simplicity of life style—characterized by very little in the way of processing steps between harvesting and consumption—scarcity of population, lack of medical attention, and poverty are always found in combination. From low productivity follow a host of miseries that are linked as cause and effect, like a parade of elephants linked trunk to tail. It is not the productivity per capita that, in starting to rise, reverses the chain of poverty. It is the productivity of the region, lifted by an increase in population, that comes first. As one telling example, it is widely believed—not without justification—that the U.S.S.R. was done in by communism. The real villain however was low population density caused by trying to spread the population over too vast an area. The result is that most Russians live in localities that do not have enough people to support high level industry or necessary public services. One consequence is that at the present time the Russian population is falling, which only exacerbates the underlying problem.

Since 1990 the rising productivity of developing nations created an abundance of commodities to fill the demands of developed nations, and at lower and lower real cost. It is not widely appreciated that even today, comparing the cost of a gallon of gasoline with the cost of a new car, the car is comparatively most expensive today than it was forty years ago, and the fuel that is the relative bargain. Under the banner of Globalization, the real cost of commodities fell throughout the 1990's thanks to quantum gains in the productivity of the developing nations and to meaningful, though more modest, gains in productivity in the commodity producing sectors of the developed countries. Gains in agricultural productivity in America and Europe in particular have been impressive.[7] They have released a large acreage of farmland for other uses, without these countries experiencing an equal decline in agricultural production. Worldwide cotton production illustrates these gains. Since 1965, acreage under cotton has not increased at all, but yields per acre have about doubled.[8] No single cause has brought this about. All over the world, today's farmers plant improved seed and spreads fertilizer over it; he has the use of modern farm implements and access to much larger markets thanks to better transportation infrastructure; he has better education and stronger health. He accomplishes more with the expenditure of less effort, making his occupation a more appealing career. The consequences of the commodity explosion, not just agriculture, are visible up to 2000 because commodity prices were falling steadily.

The steep rise in the commodity index after 2001 is therefore quite shocking, and does not by any means indicate a sudden turn in the availability of commodities. The suddenness of the reversal owes principally to world politics, rather than economics, and to a single commodity: crude oil. The price of a barrel of West Texas crude—the benchmark variety captured in crude oil futures—has exploded from about $15 to $70 per barrel. The largest beneficiary of this boom has been the Persian Gulf states, with Russia, Iran and the rest of OPEC, and Texas well owners bringing up the rear. Even the tag end of this parade are driving in style. This is by no means an unfortunate turn of events for the American administration for several reasons. Leaving aside the gratitude of Texans, the Arabian princes also have reason for gratitude, and support for America as it makes war in their neighborhood. They show their gratitude by lending much of the proceeds back to us. The roundtrip of petrodollars, from the motorist—not only American by the way—to the Persian Gulf, and then back to the U.S. Treasury in exchange for Treasury bonds works in the short term like taxes, with the further advantage that it is a tax levied on every motorist in the world, and not just on the American public. I touched on this dynamic in a previous chapter, where I pondered the widening trade deficit and its causes. The story as it applies to crude oil and to refined gasoline are not in principle any different from the broader one, but crude oil dominates the actual dollar flows.

Thus the price explosion of crude oil and gasoline is in the short run principally an indication of political relationships: the desire to placate the Persian Gulf states and at the same time to fuel their purchase of our stocks and bonds. It has a lasting effect however on the purchasing power of the dollar which will tend to make the new higher prices permanent.

Defending the Dollar

The natural reaction of the Fed, seeing the dollar threatened, is to come to its defense; to tighten the money supply and let interest rates rise. In the past our central bankers had the best of all possible worlds. They enjoyed the benefits of easy money while pursuing a strong dollar policy. What made that possible was the reserve status of the dollar. Everyone with money—whether petrodollars or trade dollars—eagerly recycled them into our markets. The accumulation of trade and fiscal deficits has undermined the logic of that choice, and the expansion of other capital markets around the globe has provided options that did not exist formerly.

What results from this is a very dangerous condition which risks a sudden, destructive deflationary crisis. Simply put, the dollar is losing value because there are more of them in central banks all over the world than they want to own. The Federal Reserve tries to staunch the decline by restraining growth of the money supply. Short term interest rates rise, which makes dollar balances more attractive, but long term rates also rise. Prices of long term notes and bonds fall, which for foreign holders only aggravates the loss caused by weakness of the dollar. Foreign investors therefore put more bonds out for the bid, and repatriate the proceeds in their own currency. Their central banks have to face the question of what to do with the surge of repatriation, which in the normal course of affairs would force them to create more money. Ultimately, the dollars will come back to the American economy, and the Fed will have to deal with them.

The Fed must choose between two courses of action: to defend the dollar or to manage its decline. It is a wise proverb that nothing succeeds like success, and it is an even wiser one that nothing succeeds like excess. The strong dollar policy has been a boon to the American consumer and to American political ends. Internationally, the status of reserve currency has greased the wheels and lowered the cost of our foreign ventures. The most natural reaction to dollar repatriation would be for the Fed to buy them with its foreign currency reserves. As long as the reserves last we could continue to live in the fantasyland of the overvalued dollar, but since no corrective steps would be taken to relieve the imbalances that are pressing on the dollar, it would be unsustainable. The alternative is a monetary policy that does not target any predetermined fixed "ideal" value of the dollar, but instead targets a preferred adjustment path. Everyone should recognize that the dollar has to decline, but no one is benefited if it collapses. The better option is an accommodative one designed to defend the stability and efficiency of the foreign exchange market. This is in essence the policy of the Peoples' Bank of China, in regard to the yuan/dollar rate. The Fed can certainly use its resources and leverage to prevent transitory market corners and panics.

At the present time, the American monetary base has been growing slowly for the last decade, and foreign central banks have compensated by aggressively extending liquidity to our economy. For the reasons stated above, it would be advisable for the Fed to ease the domestic money supply. Equally important, it is advisable that foreign central banks not hit the brakes. There has been excessive expansion of liquidity worldwide, starting with the Russia debt crisis in 1998. The commodity rally is the natural consequence of too much money chasing too few barrels and tons of stuff. Commodities are not the enemy. The world can survive almost any amount of commodity inflation. It is no service to anyone to drive the world economy into recession or depression in order to avoid it.

The example of the Great Depression is sobering, as an example of the subordination of financial and business judgments to political exigencies. The tight money policy that the Fed pursued, and that drove the American economy into crisis, were understood at the time to be economically foolish,[9] but other goals intervened. One friendly power after another began to shake—the general strike in Britain, the loss of political legitimacy of the French regime, leading to the popular front government, and the civil war in China which opened the way to Japanese imperialism—subordinated domestic monetary policy. In retrospect we see very clearly the mistakes of judgment made by the Federal Reserve, but we could not see them at the time because they were understood to be compromises forced by circumstances.

At the present time it seems very disagreeable to have to live with some of the results of commodity inflation. By enriching producers of commodities, it weakens our influence over them, and should they coordinate their decisions it puts our interests at risk. Perhaps it is regrettable that we can no longer keep them rich and docile, but it is the lesser of the available evils.

Implications for the Stock Market

Anything that shakes the value of the dollar has implications for stock markets too. In fact, the worst excesses of the strong dollar regime have been manifested in equity valuations.

For the most part, central banks do not invest directly in stock markets, but other agencies of their governments do, and they do so in quantity. Of the roughly fifteen trillion dollars of aggregate market value in all American stocks, direct foreign investment by national agencies accounts for more than one trillion. Foreign financial institutions that are highly suggestible by the financial polices of their governments have invested additional trillions in our markets. Japan, China, Singapore, and Saudi Arabia stand out as countries that are particularly highly invested.

Turning debt into equity—inducing foreign creditors to take investment positions in lieu of cash—is potentially a way to circumvent the painful adjustment that looms over the dollar, but this is an extremely short-sighted option. It is the option of choice for Britain, which is far more heavily indebted than America is, and buried under far, far more debt than they could ever possibly service. It seems that every week brings another story of a jewel sold to foreign creditors. The most recent one is the London Stock Exchange. The City of London—the financial district that accounts for everything of value in England—has been sold off to pay debts. Well, perhaps I am assuming too much. We *hope* the proceeds have been applied to the debt, although the limits of profligacy are indeed high.

The problem with selling business or industrial assets is that a foreign buyer has little or no incentive to invest in them or to develop them. The most marketable corporate assets are the bluest of the blue chips. They have market presence and name recognition that can only be built over many years of rather consistent success. The other assets of the ongoing business are however of far less value to any foreign acquirer, because they duplicate assets that he has or wants to build closer to home. An example makes this clear. Anyone, any foreign resident corporation, that bought Boeing Aerospace would be delighted to get that legendary name and product lineup, including a huge installed base of Boeing jets owned by airline carriers all over the world. It would also inherit a large, and sometimes profitable, government business in the U.S. and space technology. All of these assets would complement the management and the technical prowess of the acquirer. The Boeing's management and technical offices, by contrast, only compete with the acquirer. While some scientists and engineers and some management—especially sales—would be valuable additions to the new owner's skill set, most by far would be superfluous. In fact, to the degree that the acquirer is beholden to the wishes of its own government, the old

Boeing management and technical staff would be redundant. In short, the new owner would have every incentive to run Boeing into the ground, milking its unique business assets but otherwise bleeding it white. Selling whole businesses is the fast way to wind up with no corporate population of our own.

Because of the excessive freedom that corporate management enjoy, freedom that is usually identified by the slogan "The Separation of Ownership and Control," investing piecemeal by means of buying shares of stock is a far less inviting way to take an equity stake in America. Foreign participation in our stock market as investors comes for the most part from a policy decision of foreign governments. The actual funds may be nominally private, but they are motivated from above. Foreign commercial interests—truly profit-seeking players—have plunged eagerly into trading and hedge funds. Over the long term, however, their position in our markets average out to a very small quantity because they simply are not investors. One would have to doubt therefore that swapping debt for shares of stock has much potential as a way of absorbing incoming dollars, and of supporting the exchange value of the dollar.

The American public has expressed its judgment of the relative merits of real property versus shares of stock, and the consensus has very strongly favored real property. For the last six years, while the stock market has languished, the housing market has sprinted. Various economic observers and commentators have focused on the housing business narrowly, without reference to the broader implications for the portfolio choices of the American public. There has been a housing boom, and more broadly a building boom, principally because the public views real property as a more promising investment than shares of stock in American corporations. It is very likely that foreign investors see the same relative investment value, and would be fairly cool to the appeal of the stock market. Our stock market has gone nowhere for years, and a succession of public trials of corporate miscreants accused of raiding the treasury does little to polish the credentials of American equities. When the Congress feels compelled to step in with new legislation like the Sarbanes-Oxley Bill, which addresses a history of failures in the auditing of financial reports, the intensity of the public outcry is inescapable. The housing boom reflects many forces, but none of them is more central than a loss of confidence in shares of publicly traded corporations.

Besides whole corporations, the other kind of equity stake that we could sell is individual real assets, e.g. land, commercial real estate, and patents and copyrights to name a few of the largest kinds. This has already happened to a startling extent, with sales to Japanese investors accounting for the largest value of transactions by far. Traditionally, people have resisted absentee landlords—to use the Irish term for it—because of the perceived asymmetry of bargaining power. When neighborhood assets—a shopping mall for instance—are owned locally, the owner's greed is tempered by his awareness that he has to live with his neighbors. When however the mall has a distant owner, the owner is much less likely to accommodate the clamor of the local people. The public naturally feel that they have lost an important measure of control over their surroundings. America is large enough that this conflict can arise when a corporation on the east coast owns a mall on the west coast, but it is far likelier to raise alarm when the remote owner is completely foreign.

Selling real assets to pay debt is routine phenomenon, and the example of Japanese investment in Radio City Music Hall and the Pebble Beach Gold Resort make the point that it has not become a problem in the eyes of the American public. Nonetheless it is the sort of issue that generates a lot of heat and smoke in less developed countries which feel the loss of control over their environment to rich and exploitative foreigners.

Conclusion

We have enjoyed the best of all possible financial worlds, in which foreign businesses and government have treated the dollar as being true wealth. They have taken dollars in exchange for real goods like automobiles and television sets. Lest we run out of dollars, they have lent the proceeds back to us so that we are always ready to buy some more. This policy only works however as long as the Federal Reserve Board defends the dollar by restricting the expansion of liquidity here at home.

That policy now however faces a crossroads, because the credibility of the assurance of solid value has come into question in many places around the world. If the Fed responds by further restricting domestic liquidity, it is very likely to cause a liquidity crisis. If nervous foreign lenders would settle for swapping debt for equity, the crisis could perhaps be avoided. Rather than justifying the current structure of currency exchange rates by Fed policy, the high value of the American dollar could be justified by reference to the real assets of the American economy. In the preceding section however I tried to throw some cold water on that hope.

The Federal Reserve Board is the best informed and most professional central bank in the world, but history provides ample evidence that they are not omniscient. Will they know when to get off the strong dollar policy, or will it explode into a worldwide liquidity crisis?

Notes

1. The World Dollar Index is an average of exchange rates, weighted by the importance of each of them in American trade flows. It attaches too much weight to a few countries, especially Canada, that have disproportionately large trade relations with the U.S., but the weights are not entirely unreasonable. Trade with America is a good indicator of how much any country participates in the world economy. In the future, as trade amongst other nations grows faster than trade with America, this will be less and less true.
2. Ominously, this phrase was coined by Voltaire at a time when his France basked in many of the same blessings that we in America enjoy today. Skeptic that he was, however, he attributed it to the fool Dr. Pangloss.
3. I owe this observation to a market letter: John Mauldin's Outside the Box. V2, no. 33; May 2006.
4. Every one of these commodities is in reality a genus of many different species. They become commodities because the species, while having very different uses, have highly correlated prices.
5. The U.S. government has contributed to this by adding to our own strategic petroleum reserve.
6. They are the raw material of the industries that process them into edible forms, but apparently the *Journal of Commerce* does not include those industries in their survey.
7. Cotton production in America has only recently started to recover from the devastation of the boll weevil. The first truly effective countermeasures—a combination of new pesticides and biochemical weapons and strict farming discipline—did not begin to have a significant impact until the late 1980's. Cotton output has soared since that time.
8. Based on data compiled by the U.S. Department of Agriculture.
9. Governor Benjamin Strong of the New York Fed, certainly the wisest of the governors, repeatedly urged moderation to avoid unsettling our markets, but he was overruled.

10

The Cost of Living
and Inflation Reconsidered

It is not hard to define inflation as an economist would use that term. Inflation is depreciation in the purchasing power of the currency. It is present when a constant stream of nominal income, or a constant nominal net worth, will not secure as high a standard of living as it previously did. If Standard of Living comprises the goods and services that this world provides for us to use and consume, then inflation is the Cost of Living.

There is a tradition that prevails amongst those who purport to measure inflation—the Bureau of Labor Statistics—that their job is to measure a certain price index which is not and does not claim to be a measure of the cost of living. That disclaimer is quite accurate for them. The Consumer Price Index is not a cost of living index. To the degree that they diverge, however, the CPI is to that degree an irrelevant artifact because the only concept of inflation that has any economic significance is the cost of living. I raise this point because the CPI has become increasingly irrelevant and misunderstood. Let me expand on this theme.

What Is the Standard of Living?

The standard of living is the sum total of all those goods and services that this world affords us mortals. Most of them could be classified under the broad heading of "consumption opportunities." The services that an automobile provides to a busy modern family, for instance, is one such consumption opportunity. The cost of living naturally includes the money cost of everything that goes into a given pattern of driving. Any increase in the money cost of the vehicle or the fuel or of repairs is inflation. On the other hand, driving more or driving a nicer car are not inflation. How that family actually uses its cars is not the Cost of living, it is the Standard of living.

There are other goods that we provide to ourselves that would not conventionally be classified as consumption, but whose cost belongs in the cost of living. Through our taxes we collectively cover the expenses of the public schools. This can not be counted by the B.L.S. as consumption because the tax levy is not a fee for service. The elderly, who no longer have need of or use for public schools, pay their share while the children who obtain all the services pay none. The cost of the schools is nonetheless part of the cost of living because the schools, and the education that they provide, are an integral part of the standard of living. In whatever way people wish to spend their money, as long as the money itself actually buys something, is a legitimate part of the standard of living. What I mean by saying "actually buys something" has to do with the logic of the allocation of resources. Since the schools have real costs—the teachers must be paid and the schools heated in winter—the public outlay is buying real resources, and the school system competes with all other economic activities for them. In effect, then, the standard of living comprises all those things and those activities that the households allocate money for. This allocation is a reality, but it is by no means entirely voluntary. Items that are financed by tax dollars impose an involuntary—though admittedly not necessarily unwelcome—allocation through the tax collections. The relevant definition of the household budget is pre-tax income, or pre-tax nominal wealth.

The Paradox of Creative Destruction

The paradox of creative destruction has tripped up nearly everyone who spends any time thinking about how we measure the National Income. It is simply this annoying question: We properly count new construction of homes in national income. More homes being erected equals more income being earned. If, therefore, our goal is to have high income, why don't we each year single out 20% of all existing homes to be demolished? The owners would have to rebuild them and that would generate more building activity. That is more income, isn't it? Or to put this in another context, why don't we cheer for tornadoes and earthquakes? While neither you nor I would be guilty of such shoddy thinking, a detailed analysis of the matter provides insight into what we mean by the Standard of living.

Our natural reaction is to deny that tearing down existing homes would actually increase national income, but that is not right. Other things being equal, the families whose homes were destroyed would attempt to build anew, and doing so would actually increase measured national income. There is no paradox here.

The paradox comes from confusing national income

with the standard of living. Consider a family that has been rendered homeless. The services of their home were part of their standard of living; they were a consumption opportunity that the family formerly enjoyed. After the wreckers leave the premises however the opportunity is now gone. The family must instead dip into its current income or—more likely—its wealth, to regain what they already had. Thus we would judge that their Cost of living had increased with no corresponding increase in their Standard of living. Alternatively, if they do not rebuild, their standard of living has declined with no corresponding reduction in their cost of living. That for them is just like inflation.

Obviously, any single event and any single family do not have a measurable impact on any statistic that is intended to reflect what is going on in the society as a whole. The concept of inflation that matters to us is an average over the whole society. Casualty losses from natural causes do not have much impact on the total. We do not ordinarily concern ourselves with accidental casualty losses because they occur at a rate that is fairly constant over time and that is in any case beyond our control, but in any case the national income accounts actually do adjust for losses. The money cost of casualty losses is deducted from income. In case the loss is insured, as long as the sum received by the insured is not counted as income while the outlay from the insurer is treated as an expense, the income accounts do not overstate the standard of living. If however the federal and state governments step up to pay for rebuilding, then national income is overstated because outlays of the government are not counted as expenses.

Hidden Inflation

The Bureau of Labor Statistics does not attempt to measure the cost of living. Their brief is to track an index of the prices of goods and services that households purchase. That task has become increasingly difficult, and even problematic, over time. Chairman Greenspan has addressed this issue many times, and my conclusion is the same as his.

There are some goods the definition of which remains fairly constant over time and that are sold directly to the public. Most foods are of this type. Some more modern conveniences are also easily priced. Kilowatt hours of electricity are in practice homogeneous, because regulation of the industry has standardized the terms of service. The average household spends only a very small portion of its pre-tax income to purchase such goods however. For many other goods, the price paid is also an indication of quantity or quality. The luxurious mansion and the humblest cottage may actually provide housing at the same price, defined as price per unit of effective service. Their selling prices are primarily an indication of quantity of service rather than economic price per unit of service. The B.L.S. is well aware of this, and it takes care to compare over time prices of equivalent versions of a thing. Since they are primarily interested in tracking change in the price level, it is not hard simply to monitor price changes of standardized units.

It is much easier for the economist to describe how prices should be measured than it is for the statisticians to actually implement it. There is no perfection in government statistics. Any residual deficiencies of the price indices are not however serious enough to raise the specter of hidden inflation. We do a tolerable job of monitoring

141

the trend of the cost of that part of our living that are bought and sold in markets. The larger problem is that this is a shrinking part of our standard of living. Taxes, which pay for a variety of goods that are provided through government at all levels, consume about the same share of household income as what we spend on goods that we buy.

Inflation in Public Goods

Since goods and services that the government buys for the public are not priced, they do not appear in any price index. They are nonetheless fully as susceptible to cost inflation as are private goods. Whenever the cost of public goods and the tax levy needed to finance them rise without a corresponding gain in the amount of service or in its quality, there is inflation. More broadly, an increase in public outlays that has no commensurate increase in the standard of living is to that degree an increase in the cost of living.

While the prices of goods we purchase have been very steady for years, public outlays on goods like education have skyrocketed. It is obviously necessary to adjust for simple measures like the number of children being educated, but in fact that number has declined over time. Per pupil outlays have grown even faster than has the total expense. If we are not getting more education per pupil, the cost of education has risen. Hardly anyone would argue that our schools are significantly better than they were in the past. Our president would undoubtedly argue that they are not nearly as good, and many would rise to second him. It is not my purpose here to critique all the public services that we receive from state and local governments, but I think few would assert that the quantity of public service has risen anywhere near as fast as has the cost, and that the difference is hidden inflation.

The entire ledger of public goods presents, it seems to me, rather less gloomy reading. Improvements in public safety, especially in cities, and the positive explosion of public amenities all have added immensely to our standard of living. The public outlays to pay for them have added to the cost of living. Where we collectively net out is something that I can not say.

Money and Taxes

In the days when most goods were private goods purchased in markets, prices were a good measure of the cost of living. Inflation was in those days a matter of too much money chasing too few goods, and that in practice it was caused by rapid and sustained growth in the monetary supply. Inflation was in those times purely a monetary phenomenon. The same holds true today for that part of household outlays, but the causes of public sector inflation are not as fully understood.

We know at least where to look. Assuming for simplicity that there is no change in the amount or quality of the public services provided, inflation is caused or permitted by whatever permits taxes to rise systematically over time.[1] As long as taxes merely grow at the same rate as price inflation—as long as the cost of public services rise only as fast as a price index—then we really have the usual sort of inflation. Certainly, as prices and wages grow in the private sector, wages will grow in the public sector and the cost of goods that the government buys will also increase. A tax increase that simply passes that cost

143

squeeze along to the ultimate payer is only a byproduct of the price inflation. There is no problem of hidden inflation in that circumstance. By the same reasoning, the cause of systematic inflation is still excessive money stimulus.

Uniquely public sector inflation can arise only when taxes can rise faster than the rate of price inflation, or in other words, when the cost of public goods is rising faster than the cost of private goods. When the cost per pupil in school rises without any corresponding improvement in education, that is a symptom of mismanagement of the schools. In the 1960's, public education was hijacked and made to serve as a vast public works project. While educational goals were not consciously compromised, they were in effect subordinated to the higher goal of employing the maximum number of persons and of paying them as well as possible, subject to the public's willingness to pick up the tab.

Under what circumstances, therefore, can tax levies rise faster than the price level? Although our income tax is nominally progressive, with the result that the average tax rate should rise as money income rises, in reality the effect of progressivity is very small. The total levy from income and payroll taxes is nearly proportional to national income. Progressivity applies at the level of the individual taxpayer: those at the top of the income ladder pay the lion's share of all income taxes. It does not follow in practice, however, that if everyone got a raise, the average tax rate would rise. Many taxes are not progressive, social security being the most obvious example. The public at large, moreover, is sure to protest any broad tax rate increase, and to demand relief which returns the average tax rate to where it started. As a first approximation it is fair to say that taxes of activities, taxes of flows of income

144

or spending, rise only as fast as income, and that they track price inflation rather than leading or causing it.

This leaves another entire category of taxes: taxes on wealth or on assets. The capital gains tax is one case of this. The real property tax that local government levies is another. The tax effect of price inflation is a third. Since the tax effect of price inflation is itself tied to the rate of price inflation, I will not dwell on it here, but will focus on the real property tax. The real property tax is a tax on the market value of land and structures. When market values rise, properties are reassessed, and unless the tax rate is lowered the tax levy rises. This dynamic is the only significant way in which taxes can rise faster than price inflation of goods, and rise faster than the money supply. This nation has experienced in recent years a rather astounding building boom, both for residences and for retail and commercial developments. At the same time, monetary policy has been fairly conservative and price inflation tame. The boom has in this case been financed by massive borrowing from overseas. The availability of money from outside the country drives real estate prices higher, without needing any contribution from domestic monetary policy. The logical sequence of events is therefore: foreign lending raises property values, higher property values result in higher property taxes, higher taxes pay for a high cost of public goods.

There is another, supplementary link between borrowing from foreign sources and public sector inflation. Since governments at all levels borrow from foreigners, the capacity to spend is not limited to the current flow of taxes. Domestic borrowing is not inflationary, because the purchasing power of the citizen who has bought a government bond is reduced by the cost of the bond. The result could be to shift the incidence of inflation from the

145

private sector, where it is tracked by the B.L.S., to the public sector, where it goes unnoticed. In that case, the overall level of inflation would in fact stay the same, but measured inflation would fall because household expenditures would fall. Borrowing from foreign sources by contrast permits a net acceleration of inflation because it does not directly reduce household expenditures on private goods, while the cost and the quantity of public goods increases.

Now, as I implied earlier, I do not assert that the total dollar cost of public goods has risen faster than the value of the public services. I do not know if there has been public inflation. Speaking as a committed curmudgeon, I am inclined to suspect that is the case, but it is purely a prejudice on my part. What we can conclude however is that inflation is not merely or entirely a monetary phenomenon anymore. We have an example of a process by which the cost of living can increase—we can collectively spend more on some goods—without any concomitant increase in the money supply as it has historically been measured. Any resulting inflation will necessarily, moreover, be hidden inflation because we simply do not track the cost of public services.

As I suggested above, the need to rethink inflation and its causes has arisen only because public goods now account for such a large component of total household outlays. In the *laissez-faire* economy of the 1920's, when our methods of tracking inflation were put in place, private expenditures were large and public ones small. Price inflation was essentially synonymous with inflation. That is no longer the case. If we as a nation are serious about measuring trends in our standard of living—which goes by the highly apoetical name of "Real GDP"—we need to broaden our observations to include all goods and to assess their unit costs to the public.

Notes

1. One special situation that must be allowed for as a transfer of some consumption opportunity from the private to the public sector. If the states were to begin to purchase medical drugs and to distribute them to the public at no cost or at a subsidized cost, taxes would rise but there would not necessarily be any increase in the cost or the standard of living.

11

Fallacies in the Measurement of Inflation

The Quality Adjustment Shuffle

It is positively unamazing how many people ask this simple question:

How can we be having so much disinflation when the price of everything is rising all the time?

There are many partial answers—many truths that each contribute to the answer—and this note deals with one of those, one that has been ignored. We call it the Quality Adjustment Shuffle, and it has been practiced regularly by the B.L.S.—under the guidance of the Federal Reserve Board—for the last ten years.

It starts with a very legitimate idea, which is that when a certain product—bed mattresses for instance—comes in a range of quality versions, they will naturally sell at different prices reflecting the difference in quality. If the sales mix of mattresses were to change over time, the average selling price of a mattress would change even without any change in the price of a mattress of constant quality. The cost of living should be adjusted correspondingly. Imagine in particular that some engi-

148

neering breakthrough lowered the cost of the highest quality mattresses. The public would rush to pay more for much higher quality. Then the average selling price of a mattress would rise even though the cost of a mattress of constant quality had actually diminished. All very logical, but not historically very relevant over the last decade.

There is another scenario. I will take the case of a single hypothetical maker of mattresses as an example. Formerly, XYZ Corp made only one kind of mattress that sold for $400. The management sees import competition growing, and pricing pressure growing with it. With some re-working of their process and using better materials, they have introduced a new line priced at $600. The BLS applies their quality adjustment math, which implies that the new mattress is 1 1/2 times as good as the old one. The reasoning is that if people who want to sleep are indifferent between the two offerings, the more expensive one must provide correspondingly more "mattress."

Now, bring on the import competition. Unit sales of the cheaper mattresses fall drastically. XYZ becomes increasingly dependent on sales of the quality mattress. But let's suppose that their costs have risen, and it is necessary to raise the price from $600 to $800. They can not raise the price of the economy mattress, because they still hope to sell some of them. We would naturally conclude that the cost of an XYZ mattress had risen a lot: nearly 33%. Since they sell primarily the quality line, their price on that line is close to their average price.

While you and we suppose that, the BLS does not suppose it. Their Quality Adjustment tells them that since XYZ Corp is still willing to sell mattresses for $400, and since both lines continue to attract some customers, the price difference is purely a reflection of quality. That is to say, the quality mattress is now twice as much "mattress" as the economy one. As long as there is any product line made by XYZ which—because of import competition—continues to sell at the old price, no price change on any of the other lines is attributed to inflation. It is all by assumption Quality Improvement.

Actually, one could go further. As sales of the economy line slump, XYZ management decides to slash the price in order to defend their sinking market share. They lower the price to $300. Now they have the two product lines: an economy line selling for $300 and a premium line selling for $800. Therefore—in BLS reasoning—the premium mattress is now equal to 2 2/3 as much mattress [i.e. $800/$300]. The quality adjusted selling price has actually *fallen* from $400 per mattress to $300 per mattress of constant quality!

So, what does this say about real product and productivity? By now everyone is aware that Gross Domestic Product adds up the dollar value of goods and services produced in America and divides by the price index. For this purpose, imports don't count, because they are obviously not part of our domestic product. In the case XYZ Corp—of its contribution to GDP—we look at sales—which is primarily sales of the premium mattress at the rate of $800 per unit—and the index of the price of their product—an index that has diminished by 25% because they have had to meet the import competition on their economy product—has fallen. When we divide output in dollars by the resulting price index, the message is that output has expanded dramatically, along with productivity. If this scenario begins to look familiar, if you think this is what has happened in industry after American industry over the last nine years, welcome to the club.

This fable, this fictional history of XYZ Corp, does not stop at this point. XYZ Corp is making fewer mattresses.

Total sales nationally of mattresses may have grown, because of imports, but in any case XYZ is making less. They make fewer economy mattresses because of the competition, and their unit output of the premium mattresses has not replaced that loss because the high price limits their market. Since, therefore, they are making fewer mattresses, they can close old factories and furlough older employees. So this is how it shapes up: more "real" output, divided by fewer employees. This "equals" even larger gains in labor productivity. It takes a remarkable act of blind faith in Alan Greenspan to believe that American workers are being laid off because they have become so much more productive than they were before.

If rising productivity causes employers to dismiss their employees—that is to say if high productivity causes unemployment—why don't the employees simply lay down on the job and take a nap rather than work? Then presumably their employers would be willing to hire more of them.

The Housing Bubble Anomaly

There are other distortions of the Consumer Price Index besides the ones noted above: that it ignores the cost of goods that we buy with our tax dollars, and that it uses unrepresentative prices of many items that have migrated to premium goods. The housing market constitutes another one.

The price of housing that figures in the C.P.I. is the house and apartment rental rates. I have already discussed the housing bubble previously, but in that context I did not explain how it distorts the C.P.I. The bubble has had two dimensions, as most people are aware: there has been an explosion of new building, and the prices of homes—new and old—have escalated. The two dimensions go hand in hand. It is the higher prices that have fed the drive to build. The escalation of prices is fueled by the explosive growth in mortgage lending, financed by foreign lenders.

New homes compete with rental units to find occupants. Growth in new housing translates immediately into lower rental rates. So this is how it works. The higher the price of new homes—meaning the higher the price of housing in the form of single family units—the lower are rental rates on existing homes and apartment units. The higher the price of houses, the lower is the price that the B.L.S. recognizes for housing!

12

Money, Gold, and Inflation

As Cautious As Croesus: Gold As an Inflation Hedge

Croesus was a king in ancient times whose vast wealth made him the standard by which other people were judged. It was a high honor to be as rich as Croesus. What made his pile so visible to an admiring public was that he accumulated it in gold, because that was for practical purposes the only financial asset available at the time. Perceptive people of that day recognized, as we do, that gold is not really wealth, but is only a kind of counter for wealth. But the convenience of the counter was enormous. A simple vault in the palace of the king could hold a fortune equal to an immense acreage of prime farmland, and the gold did not bring with it hordes of recalcitrant peasants, unpredictable weather, and leaf blight. Gold, like other financial assets, is a form of wealth which requires very little active management by the possessor, at least in comparison to any form of so-called real wealth. For that reason it is unique in being the centerpiece of the gold standard, which is again the talk in financial circles.

Gold is only one of many financial assets today. Individuals rarely hold a significant fraction of their wealth in this form, but it is one which serves as a hedge against inflation in fiat money. Alan Greenspan is said to watch the price of gold closely, for signs of market sentiment on inflation and deflation. The insurance that it provides is effective, though expensive. A present-day Croesus would be more cautious than rich.

Gold and Inflation: Some Theory

There are two essential characteristics which an inflation hedge must have. The first and most obvious one is that over long intervals of time its real value should be much less variable than its nominal value, or in other words its real value should be highly predictable off into the distant future. As an ideal, we might say that the real value should be constant, although strictly speaking that would probably be impossible to achieve. It is permissible for an inflation hedge to earn a real rate of return—i.e., for the real value to grow steadily over time; but if the asset is, like gold, essentially riskless, the real rate of return should be small. In any case, positive and negative real rates of return have to be transitory. It would be better for the expected rate of real return, which in the case of gold is the same as the rate of change of the real price, to be absolutely zero forever. Many investments which are pretty good inflation hedges, such as farmland and commercial real estate, earn a significant real return as well, but that is because they entail a lot of specific investment risk.

The degree to which the real price of gold has been constant over time is truly remarkable, as the accompanying graph shows. This graph is our *Logistic Centerfold* for the month of February 2000.[1] Our February centerfold has an affinity for gems, does important work in the medical field, and thinks platinum is "too too." Beyond that,

Real Dollar Gold Price

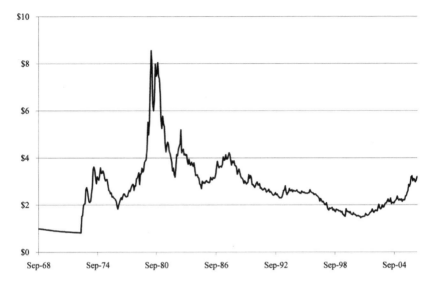

Source: CPI: U.S. Department of Labor and Logistic Research & Trading Co.; Gold: Handy & Harmon afternoon fixing.

she coyly declines to be interviewed, but in any case the picture speaks for itself. It covers the period from 1946, when the price of gold was fixed at $35 per oz., to 2006, a span of 60 years. In order to clarify the overall trend, I have taken annual averages, leaving 60 data points. "The" price of gold at each point is simply the average over the year, deflated by the CPI.

While gold has varied in real terms, the net change over the period is rather small, as the graph shows and the following simple calculations confirm. At the end of May, 1999, gold was selling for about $260 per oz. If it had simply risen with inflation, starting in 1932, the price would have been $430 per oz. If one test of an inflation

155

hedge is the predictability of its real value, this is a pretty creditable performance. There are not many factors which one could forecast 67 years ahead and come within about 40% of the actual result. The price of gold has fallen precipitously this year, and if we used an average price—the average price that appears on the graph as the last column—the real price of gold has fallen only about 20% over a span of 67 years.

It is tempting to delve into the unique factors that have influenced the price of gold over various subintervals of this history. The recent years, in particular, have been colored by two bearish events: the creation of a unified European currency that is a new, highly credible reserve currency, and also a runaway increase in mine production. The creation of the new Euro is probably already familiar, though what has happened to gold mine production probably is not. This decade has actually witnessed the greatest gold rush in history. It would be a mistake, however, to interpret these sorts of events as in some way an exception to the rest of history. There are always good fundamental economic reasons for why the real price of gold is stable in the long run. It is the microeconomic forces of production costs and demand for gold jewelry, among other factors, that eventually have to do the heavy lifting of keeping the real price in line.

While the high predictability of gold's real value probably may come as something of a surprise, the overall shape of the history surely comes as no surprise to anyone from the baby boom generation. Gold first rallied after President Nixon closed the gold window in 1971. Even though the years surrounding the relaxation of the Nixon price controls were a time of high inflation, gold soared even faster, and by 1975 it had made up all the ground lost between 1932 and 1971. This sequence was repeated in the second half of the decade, with gold finally peaking in January, 1980. It closed at $850 per oz. on January 21st. Since then, gold has slid pretty steadily in real value, except for a short-lived rally in 1987. There is little evidence that we have reached a bottom of the bear market. The nominal price is lower today—at $260—that it has been at any time in the last twenty years.

There is no denying that within the period there were times of very large positive and negative real returns. Surprisingly, their existence does not invalidate the proposition that gold is an inflation hedge. On the contrary, these large returns are necessitated by the rules of how an inflation hedge works. This is tied up in the second essential characteristic of an inflation hedge.

Gold and Unexpected Inflation

The idea that the real value of an inflation hedge should be roughly constant over time is easily accepted, and seems to be true almost by definition. What is less obvious is that when inflation accelerates, an inflation hedge must outpace it, and conversely when inflation slows, the hedge must slow even more. In other words, an inflation hedge must have a positive expected real rate of return in inflationary periods and a negative expected real rate of return in disinflationary times.

An asset which simply followed inflation would provide insurance against inflation only up to the amount invested in that asset. At that rate, gold would be a diversifier of risk—by hedging up a part of the total portfolio—but it would not be a hedge asset for the whole portfolio. An inflation hedge must generate gains and losses to offset inflationary losses and disinflationary gains on the rest of the portfolio. It does so by realizing a positive real rate of return when inflation accelerates, and correspondingly a negative real rate of return when it decelerates. The cumulative real rate of return over long periods of time will net out to zero, as it did over the last sixty years, if episodes of unexpected inflation and unexpected disinflation net out.

It is possible, using the last twenty years of data, to be more precise about how much gold one would need to hedge a portfolio. There is no single universal answer to this question because it depends on the specifics of the portfolio and on the investor's investment horizon. It is obvious, for instance, that you need more gold to hedge a portfolio of long term bonds than to hedge a portfolio of commercial real estate, because real estate rentals adjust to inflation. The relationship between gold and inflation, however, is the same regardless of what else any particular investor has in his portfolio, and so it is possible to get a fairly definite answer to that part of the analysis.

Over the last twenty years, the empirical rule has been that gold rallies about 5% for every 1% that the inflation rate accelerates, and symmetrically that gold falls about 5% for every 1% drop in inflation. The changes in inflation referred to here are one-time-only changes in the cost of living, and the associated change in the price of gold is also a one-time-only event. If instead the added 1% of inflation was *permanent*—with prices rising indefinitely by an added 1% *each year*—gold would also have to rise 5% every year. Stepping back from the brink of endless inflation, let's fix on a single, one-time-only 1% rise in the CPI. A 1% rise in the Consumer Price Index would lower the real value of any bond or note which matures more than one year in the future. Since the note would be paid in dollars which are worth 1% less, its present—and

158

therefore totally "real"—value would also drop by 1%. Using the 5% rule quoted above, to hedge a portfolio of bonds and notes, one would want to own $1 of gold for every $5 of fixed income assets.

Bonds and notes are of course unique in as much as the real cost of inflation on their value is entirely governed by the nature of the security itself. Any other asset, whose future cash payouts can float more or less cleanly with inflation, would require further detailed analysis and quantification, which we cannot attempt here. It seems safe to say as a general rule however that other assets are less impacted by inflation than bonds are, so gold should constitute somewhat less than 1/6th of any investment portfolio.

It may seem unfair of us to recall beleaguered Croesus at this point, because he was presumably not thinking of hedging inflation when he laid up his store of gold, and he has already endured centuries of scorn as the lead character in the story of King Midas. In his defense, gold performed financial services which we obtain today in other, more efficient ways. Nonetheless, it is impossible to let him off without noting that he was a good *six times* as cautious as a prudent investor needs to be.

The Gold Standard

Proponents of a gold standard like to point to the hedging properties of the metal as the rationale for a gold standard. The premise is of course that if gold holds in real value over time—which it does—and that if a nation wanted its currency to do the same, it should make a firm contractual tie between the two.

Speaking only for myself, I have very little interest in

this idea, and I think that most investors would feel the same. The only things that are really important are that *gold* be on the gold standard and that it be available to the investing public. At one time or another, the sponsors of nearly every other currency have promised that their brand would be just as good as gold. This note of skepticism should in no way, however, diminish the real achievements of that noted gold bug at the Fed.

Note

1. This piece first appeared in February 2000, as a newsletter to Logistic Customers. I have updated the data to 2006.

13

A Proposal on Tax Policy

The matter of taxation is so immense that it fills libraries. Taking this topic at its broadest, the only bit of advice that I would care to advance is that the reasoning of Milton Friedman has always proved to be wise and illuminating, and that anyone who wants to master this field could do much worse than to begin with his writings on this subject. My only modest goal here is to present one small suggestion on tax policy, having to do with the category of tax exempt entities. What I propose I can summarize in a single observation:

Every organization that delivers a service and that charges for its services is a business, and should be treated like every other business. The only sense in which they are not-for-profit is when in fact they do not make any money—the auto industry springs to mind on this score—in which case they don't actually owe any taxes.

There truly are not-for-profit entities. State and local governments are non-profit organizations. Charitable and religious entities that depend on donations from the public are also. Gifts to a charity and donations to a church are not compensation for service rendered. Without doubt, the generous parishioner derives benefits from

161

his church and from his participation in its activities, but in any true church, these rewards are provided free, as a matter of duty. A church that "sells" its services by threatening to withhold them until suitable compensation has been rendered is not a church; it is a business. However, all or nearly all entities that actually claim a religious mission are true non-profits: distributing their work to their congregations as a matter of a higher duty.

Most organizations that are accorded not-for-profit status by the Internal Revenue Service enjoy this designation legitimately. By number, I'm sure that the single largest number are charitable trusts created under a will and expending their income to further the goal designated by the testator. There are however many true businesses that lurk in the not-for-profit [501–C–9] category and as a rule these are the biggest organizations. Every hospital provides services to the public and charges for them. The fact that some hospitals, and other care facilities, operate on a for-profit basis demonstrates what is their true economic nature. Every school, college, and university also sells its services, and again there are many for-profit schools that makes this point very clearly. In practice, when it comes to assigning individual operations to for-profit or not-for-profit status, there will always be difficult, grey cases. I can only be thankful that I do not have to deal with them. But the giant medical centers, the Mayo Clinics for example, are not ambiguous cases; they are clearly business. The change I will propose would necessitate a rethinking of the tax status of every enterprise that is not-for-profit at this time, but in the following discussion I will limit my focus to hospitals. They present both an example of the broader proposition, and as a group they account for a very large share of the capital that is tied up in the non-for-profit sector. Just getting the treatment of hospitals right would in practice therefore achieve a large share of the total reform I am suggesting.

The origin of not-for-profit treatment of hospitals and similar facilities is intimately tied to the history of modern medicine. In the distant past, hospitals were primarily places where the sick and the injured stayed while they recuperated. Treatment was limited and the emphasis was on palliative care. A hospital a century ago was rather similar to a nursing home or an assisted living facility for the elderly. As a result, the hospital was a very labor-intensive operation. The successive revolutions in medicine have produced an ambitious treatment industry that has become highly capital-intensive. Not-for-profit status of hospitals was created as a vehicle to subsidize the heavy investment demands of modern medicine. A second rationale was advanced, which is that hospitals provide some purely charitable care for which they are not paid. In fact however the growth of medical insurance—both private pay and government pay—has diminished the scope of truly charitable services to near zero, with the exception of emergency care.[1] When individuals paid for their own hospitalization, charity was a form of rough-and-ready socialized medicine. When the services of the hospital were limited and relatively inexpensive that worked well enough, but today it is not feasible to ask hospitals and clinics to assume the financial risk of truly charitable—non-paying—care. Hence we expect very little actual charity, and we expect the government to pay when the patient cannot.

The rationale that survives, then, is the one I identified above: the desire to subsidize investments made by hospitals in medical equipment and technologies. That justification has rather interesting peculiarity: we do not

163

subsidize other investment by for-profit enterprises. In fact, it is precisely the return on investment by the Ford's and Microsoft's of the world that constitute the "profit" that we are so eager to tax. Not-for-profit status is therefore a subsidy to the enterprises that enjoy it, and simultaneously a burden imposed on investment of every other kind.[2] It is impossible to subsidize every hyperbaric operating theater without simultaneously taxing every computer-integrated control system in a Ford plant. Subsidies are like see-saws. It never happens that both sides rise simultaneously. The cost of distorting investment decisions in this way is not the only serious consequences of according not-for-profit status to hospitals and similar enterprises.

There is one essential difference between a for-profit enterprise and a not-for-profit one: someone owns the profit-making business, but no one owns the not-for-profit. The not-for-profit has a nominal owner, which is some trustee or board of trustees, but they are not beneficial owners. The members of the board are only functionaries entrusted with the task of seeing to it that the terms of the trust which created the enterprise are honored. If the hospital actually earned a profit—in reality a very common event—the profit does not belong to anyone. It remains on deposit with the trust but it cannot be paid out. Either the funds remain on deposit or they are expended to buy something that is consistent with the mission of the enterprise. In other words, they are reinvested in it: to buy more hyperbaric operating theaters and more M.R.I.'s, or to build a new wing on the facilities, or to build a new doctors' building.[3]

Since in fact the hospital is profitable because the capital goods it invests in are profitable, its accumulated capital can only grow. It can never declare a dividend because there is no one who would be entitled to claim it. Not-for-profit treatment has created for hospitals and other similar caring institutions something like the Sorcerer's Apprentice dilemma. You will recall that the sorcerer's apprentice waited until his master had gone off on a journey, and then he simply had to try out some of the spells and incantations he had committed to memory. The very first spell was cast on a salt mill that produced salt from nothing. So in no time, the mill was spewed forth free salt. It was only then that the apprentice began to realize that he had learned the incantation to start the mill, but he had not learned the spell to stop it. The parallel is this: through tax exempt status, we have started favored businesses saving and reinvesting in themselves, but now we don't know how to stop them from reinvesting endlessly. Obviously, nothing goes on forever. Some witty legislator will find a way to give the I.R.S. access to the capital of hospitals, but already the mindless logic of tax exemption has caused those favored enterprises to grow far beyond the economic logic of their markets and to load themselves with more facilities than they need.

From time to time, specialists in medical economics and public policy convene to confer amongst themselves on the subject of how to stop overinvestment in medical facilities. Since they do not stop to question the role of tax exemption however, the outcome is usually to reach for quick fixes. They have forgotten that the business world long ago figured out how to direct investment capital to its most productive uses. What is required is to rely on private property.[4]

The Proposal

The terms of what I suggest are easily stated. The steps can be listed in order:

1. Remove tax-exempt status from every enterprise that provides services to the public and charges for its services. Every enterprise of that kind is a business, just like every other business.

2. Require that the business—a community hospital for instance—be sold to a taxable business organization which has an owner or owners. In the case of a large enterprise like the Mayo Clinic, this would probably be done by issuing shares of stock in the new corporation.

3. The proceeds of this sale would then be the sole asset of the trust fund that formerly owned and operated the hospital. How that wealth would be used is something for its board to decide, but presumably it would be transformed into a foundation dedicated to promoting good health. They could buy some of the shares of the new corporation—the hospital—but they would have no participation in the management. The corporation would be answerable equally to all its investors.

4. The new foundation could retain its tax-exempt status or not, depending on the will of the I.R.S. and of the Congress that establishes its policies. If public exigencies demanded a raid on the pool of money, some compromise would be suggested. In any case, the fate of the old trust—the new foundation—is not the focus of this proposal.

Now the new hospital corporation would invest in itself on the same terms that Ford Motor and Microsoft invest in themselves. It would no longer be forced by law to reinvest every penny of net income regardless of the investment merits. If no worthwhile opportunity presented itself, the management could always return the surplus to the investors, to spend or invest as they might see fit.

Would This Change Medicine Today?

That question is much too broad for this forum, but there is one aspect of it that is both very topical and that we can say something about. A portion of the public are understandably fearful of the advent of "corporate medicine," meaning medical care delivered by profit-making business. They fear that needed care will be denied them because it is not profitable. This danger is especially imputed to medical insurance, which has a narrow incentive to economize by denying coverage.

These fears are by no means unjustified, but there is another side of the story. The greatest single change in medicine today is the advent of what is called "Information Based Medicine." In the past, doctors were forced by necessity to make rather uninformed decisions about treatment because so little was known about how effective particular courses of treatment really are and under what patient circumstances they are actually indicated. That is changing, and the change over just the last twenty years has been extraordinary. We now know so much about, to take one example, who would probably benefit from back surgery and who would not.

There is much less guesswork involved in deciding on surgery in any given case. It is inevitable that some sufferers who are poor risks will complain that surgery is being denied them just to save money. It is equally possible that some insurers will complain that their money is being wasted on unnecessary and fruitless surgery. In the past, when this sort of dispute arose, there was no way to weigh the facts and to judge based on them rather than on emotional grounds. Over time the amount of information available in medicine will only grow, because we have made reporting outcomes an integral part of medical practice. Hand in hand with the growth of knowledge, the legitimacy and the impartiality of treatment decisions will only grow.

Notes

1. Amongst hospitals, the major medical centers continue to offer some charitable treatments in unusual cases that the medical staff—usually university faculty—want to gain experience in. The beneficiaries rarely and only accidentally live near the hospital, and the selection of cases owes more to medical research than to charity.
2. Not-for-profit status has grown layers of complexity that tax the credulity of sensible persons, but these complications actually only broaden and deepen the investment subsidy.
3. The new doctors' building is a subsidiary of the hospital, but it is not tax exempt. It reports profits and pays taxes, but this does not solve the problem, because its profits after tax are simply returned to the Trust, to be reinvested in some other permitted activity.
4. This was the thesis of one of the single greatest essays in the history of economic thought: Frank H. Knight. Some Fallacies in the Interpretation of Social Cost. *Quarterly Journal of Economics* 38 (1924): 582–606. In that essay, Professor Knight explained definitively the function of private property in the allocation of scare resources.

14

Redefining Shares:
A Plan to Return Corporate
Control to the Owners

Introduction

Since the time of Gardner Means, economic theory has struggled with the separation of ownership and control that lies at the heart of modern corporate structure. Finance theory, that branch of economic thought most directly involved in sorting out this issue, has a history of ignoring the separation of ownership and control—seemingly dismissing it as a holdover of antiquated Marxian economics—but in recent years finance has also finally awakened to it. The finance perspective is that it is a problem of correctly aligning incentives for the management, under the heading of the principal—agent problem. This line of attack has proved somewhat fruitful, but the separation of ownership and control remains. Modern accounting has also struggled with this issue in its own way. Certainly the accountants could not be accused of ignoring the problem. Quite the opposite, accounting exists, and has existed from ancient times, to create and enforce accountability between principals and agents. Yet the separation of ownership and control has proved to be a hardy weed that survives and perhaps thrives despite these attacks.

Governance of modern corporations rests on a paradox. It is necessary to give management very wide latitude in directing the business affairs of the corporation, but this freedom seems inevitably to confer a freedom to exploit providers of capital. The investors as a group are very remote from the decisions that shape the corporation and that create the profits on their investment, and they are not expert enough either to make those decisions or to judge them. Even the scantiest sample of annual proxy ballots reveals that shareholders have little say in the decisions that directly impact the value of their rights, because only the most superficial matters are presented to a vote of the shareholders. Creditors of the corporation have of course even less input, but at least their interests are protected by contractual promises. In this note I will focus on the problem facing the equity shareholders, which is that shareholders cede very broad discretion to the professional management. In fact, investors would not want to have control even if that was feasible because the management was hired precisely to use that freedom in the best interests of the investor-owners.

Accounting statements presumably give the owners regular reports on the outcomes produced by the management, but this information has limited value since the shareholders have few options when it comes to interpreting the statement, and even fewer options for dealing with the management. The tools of accounting are finely tuned to detect outright fraud or theft on the part of the employees but they are not very insightful when it comes to differentiating between incompetence, bad luck, and subtler forms of larceny. One dislocation that intervenes between ownership and management is however easy to address, and that is the Ponzi scheme through which management claims to have made money by way of reported earnings, but also conveniently explains that no money is available to the investors because everything has been reinvested in the business.

This is a very widespread practice. One of the more egregious instances offers a gripping example of the whole species. Digital Equipment Corp was organized, according to corporate legend, in 1958 in Kenneth Olsen's garage. There is no questioning his genius with computers, and the company grew rapidly. But all good things come to an end. By 1993, a succession of failed projects and aggressive competition from integrated circuits sounded the death knell of the firm. It was disposed of in parts, and the proceeds paid out to the shareholders. Over the course of thirty-five years, Digital Equipment had grown at one point to be the second largest computer maker, and its native operating systems—VAX-VMS—was generally acknowledged to be the most powerful operating system available. Despite this, the company never paid a dime of dividends, and the rate of return to any shareholder who bought into the initial offering and waited for the proceeds of the dissolution was very meager. The gap between reported profits and actual distributions to the shareholders was a yawning chasm. Digital's history is by means a unique instance. It would be possible to multiply similar instances, especially in the computer and related businesses, where reported earnings seem in hindsight to have been a fiction.[1]

One thing that certainly needs to be done is to hone accounting standards to narrow the gap between real and reported earnings. The accounting profession undertook a significant reform of this sort with the new treatment it proposed for employee stock options. Investors applaud that reform, even though the S.E.C. and the Congress have moved to block it, so gifts of stock options to the management are still treated as without cost to the issuer. The incentive that impels management to lie about earnings however is very powerful, and will not go away as a result of any action by the accounting profession. What I propose in this regard is rather fundamentally different.

Whose Earnings Are They?

The greatest fallacy in corporate governance today is that the management should be the final arbiter of both reported earnings and dividends. Specifically, the Board of Directors of each corporation takes two actions each quarter: it acknowledges the audited report of profits for the most recent quarter, and it votes a dividend payout for the current quarter. There is a theory in finance that dividends don't matter, on the thesis that the management uses retained earnings—the difference between reported earnings and dividends paid—to invest in projects at least as profitable as the ones that shareholders might see elsewhere. The evidence demonstrates otherwise.

One sort of contrary evidence is that corporations do not live forever, and yet in most instances the management continues to reinvest retained earnings in the business. In rare instances the business disappears because it has been bought on advantageous terms by a larger rival, but more often the business either is disposed of or sold on disadvantageous terms. Clearly, managements are very inclined to reinvest the owners' money in very poor prospects; investment that will very likely earn a negative rate of return.

The other contrary evidence is that historically the lion's share of the total return on common stock has come from the dividend.[2] This implies that on average, management reinvests retained earnings at a rate of return significantly lower than the shareholders could have gotten on their own. Yet management persists in treating the profit of the business as if it was their property rather than the property of the owners. This tendency has moreover worsened very appreciably over time, and the dividend yield of the S&P 500 universe has fallen from 5% or better in the 1950's to about 1.5% today. I will comment later on the implications of this trend for the stock market. Right now my focus is on the rights of shareholders.

The reported profit of the corporation is an estimate of how much the owners of the business could take and spend without diminishing its future earning potential. The Internal Revenue Code has historically given the owners a tax incentive to reinvest the profits in the business. Even though the value of this incentive has been steadily reduced over time, the fraction of reported profits that are—presumably—reinvested has not diminished. Quite obviously there is no alternative to accepting the earnings report presented by the management, subject to outside audit. By the same token however, there is no reason whatsoever to accept management control of the dividend payout. There is another way:

Let the management report earnings per share. Following that, each shareholder has the option to take part or all of the asserted earnings in cash dividend. The remainder would be reinvested in the corporation.

The mechanics of this process are really very simple.

173

Each year at some pre-specified date selected by management, all outstanding shares of the corporation would be redeemed by the corporation and replaced by new shares with $1 per value. The redemption price would be $1 plus reported profits per share. As long as profit per share is positive, the shareholder can take cash up to his share of reported earnings—in which case he received the same number of shares as he tendered—or he can take less cash and correspondingly more new shares. If the management reports a loss, the total number of new shares issued is less than the old shares tendered by the amount of the loss, at the rate of $1 per share. The shareholder can not claim any cash from the corporation—I do not want to create a leverage engine—but he has the option of selling shares in the stock market.

The discipline this provides comes from the fact that any shareholder who perceives that management had overstated earnings per share would have the option of calling them on their claim by taking the cash. At the same time, the investor has the opportunity to reinvest in the business by taking his payout in shares—at $1 per share—rather than in cash. It is not up to the management and their Board to decide how much to reinvest. That decision is left entirely to the investor.

Tax Consequences

The present tax treatment of corporate profits amounts to a very high tax rate because corporate profits are in effect taxed three times: first as corporate income, then as capital gains, and finally as personal taxes on dividends. Recently the federal government lowered the tax rate on dividends received by individuals, which is of course a desirable move, but it is not enough. The high tax rate on dividends paid out has been used as justification by managements which do not want to pay dividends, and as such it has helped to provide cover for inflated earnings by severing the natural bond between profits and dividends.

The change I propose would do little to alleviate the high tax rate on corporate profits, but it would eliminate the additional confusion that comes from the treatment of capital gains. Assuming no change in the tax code, the individual taxpayer would pay income taxes on any dividend distributions he takes during the year. The incentive to retain profits comes from the deferment of taxes on retained profits. In today's world, if corporation A reports—claims—to have earned $1 per share but retains it, the taxable investor pays no tax immediately. The taxable shareholder pays no tax on reinvested profits. The rationale is that the shareholder can only be levied in relation to the "ability to pay," which means in practice that without cash with which to pay, no tax is due. Where cash is deferred, the tax liability is also deferred. This is the existing practice, according to which no taxes are due on the appreciated value of shares until they are sold. It is not the business of the Internal Revenue Code to force investment decisions of individuals by forcing them to sell shares in order to pay taxes.

When a taxable shareholder sells shares he pays tax on the realized gain. If the shares were purchased in the stock market, the gain equals the selling prices minus the cost of the shares that he designates. Since shares acquired from the corporate treasury in lieu of cash dividend have no accounting cost, their cost basis is zero.[3] When they are sold, the realized gain is equal to the entire selling price. Under rules that give the shareholder the power to claim the profits attributed to his shares, the same deferment of a part of reported profits would still exist. The only differences would be that retained earnings would not inflate the price of existing shares; they would increase the number of shares outstanding. More importantly however, the decision to retain reported profits would be in the hands of the investor, rather than the entrenched management. While this plan would not change any tax liability, the corporation would find that by treating the investors fairly, its cost of capital would be lower. At present, retained earnings seem to be a cheap source of financing because it is a way for the management to hijack the profits. This is shortsighted, however, because it overlooks how the market value of the business is depressed as a result. Treating the investors fairly is the right way to achieve a lower cost of capital.

For taxable investors, as long as the value of new shares they receive is not taxed until those shares are sold, there would be no tax consequence of this plan. If the value of new shares was taxed immediately—making it necessary for the investor to sell some of them to pay the tax—his tax liability would rise. Even in this event however, taxable investors own only a small fraction of all shares. For most equity investors it would make no difference at all. It would obviously have no impact on truly tax-exempt investors, which includes all college endowments, charitable trusts, and fund balances of not-for-profit businesses like community hospitals. It would also have no effect on retirement accounts, even though they are owned by individuals and businesses that pay taxes on ordinary income. All taxes on corporate and public pension plans, and similarly all taxes on personal I.R.A.'s, are deferred. For an individual with shares of stock in his I.R.A., it would make no difference in his taxes because returns on assets in his I.R.A. are not included in ordinary income. He pays taxes—at a high rate because it is ordinary income—only when he draws from his account, and all that matters at that time is how successful the chosen investments have been.

This discussion of taxes assumes that reported profits are positive—so that the investor can take cash and incur a tax liability. If profits are zero or negative, the investor does not have the option to take any cash, and thus of course there can not be a liability.

Underreporting of Profits

The change I propose is designed to reduce the incentive to overstate profits, but on the face of it nothing prevents the corporation for understating profits. It might seem that management can avoid paying out profits to the investors by the simple expedient of reporting that it earned no profits. Management has however very little reason to underreport profits, because doing so only diminishes the record of their performance. They are not going to be rewarded very generously for systematically hiding profits. Underreporting profits is moreover a crime which, if detected by the Internal Revenue Service, will send the management to prison. A corporation that persistently underreported its profits would also dodge a portion of its taxes due. A corporation that persistently underpays corporate income tax had better not be hiding positive profits. It is not beyond the realm of possibility that the I.R.S. might actually wink at underreporting, especially if the corporation kept separate books for calculating income taxes. In that case, it would be necessary for the investors to impose a rule that reported earnings could never be less than the after-tax profits implied by the actual income reported to the I.R.S., and to the taxes paid, i.e. the profits that would justify actual taxes payable.

It is worthwhile all the same to think through the implications of underreporting and of overreporting for the price of a share of stock. It is a given that reported profits or losses are in fact only an estimate of actual economic profits, and that as a result the report is sure to be, after the fact, an overestimate or an underestimate. It is possible moreover that some canny investors will actually be able to measure profits more accurately than the management, and will correctly perceive some of the gap. For the present however I will assume that the rational investor possessing generally available information has no reason not to accept reported profits, even though he is aware that with more precise insight into the workings of the corporation he might have a better estimate. Note in particular that he reasons that the I.R.S. is satisfied that profits are not underreported.

Details of the Shareholder's Choice

The shareholder's choice of cash or new shares depends on several factors, but only one of them is connected to the shares. If he expects the price of existing shares to be greater than $1 the moment after profits are reported, he would be better off taking the shares. If the price of a share will fall below $1, barring tax consequences for the moment, he would be better off taking the cash. These are quite unambiguous rules—again, barring tax consequences—because he can always convert shares into cash or vice versa.

Why would shares trade above or below par value after profits are known? The relationship between the market value of shares and the par value of $1 depends on how the expected rate of return compares with the cost of capital of the firm. At the moment when profits for the preceding year are reported, the shares can still trade above par if the investors expect the company to earn on average a rate of return above its cost of capital. Stepping back a day in time, before profits were reported, the shares would have been priced at approximately the sum of expected profits and the after-reported price.[4] This equation among expectations is actually a tautology, of the form:

Pre-report price per share = expected post-report price + expected profit per share.

The choice between the cash dividend and additional new shares depends on several factors that are entirely unique to each shareholder, things like his need for current income and the tax consequences of his choice. Leaving those aside, the choice depends on whether the expected post-report price is greater than or less than $1. If the investor perceives that the corporation's rate of return on investment is above its cost of capital, he will be inclined to take the shares. If the perceived rate of return falls short of the cost of capital, he would be inclined to take the cash. He may not actually have *ex post* the option of cash, if the corporation lost money, but in any case he would express his choice of cash in preference to new shares *ex ante*. There are three distinct scenarios to consider: that the expected post-report price is above par value; that it is below par value but profits for the last year were positive; and that the expected post-report

179

price is below par value and the corporation lost money in the preceding year.

If the expected price after profits are reported is greater than $1, no rational investor would take any dividend payout. All profits will be retained by the corporation, and presumably reinvested in their business. Since they earn a return on investment above their cost of capital—above the expected rate of return of competing investment opportunities—that is the optimal outcome. This is true even if they report a loss, and were expected to report a loss. A successful corporation can report a loss for a year if its true economic profits are embedded in asset revaluation for which there is no immediate tax liability and which are not immediately reflected in income. In any case however there is no need for an explanation. It is always better to take the shares, at par value, than to take cash.

As long as the margin between the corporation's expected return and their cost of capital remains, the shares will be priced consistently above par. Business opportunities are not limitless however, and as the corporation expands and ultimately exhausts its preferred endeavors, its rate of return will tend to revert to the level of its cost of capital. The attenuation of the premium of its shares will moreover be accelerated by the continual dilution. The constant par value—which I have taken to be $1 for simplicity—provides a very visible benchmark for every investor and for the management to judge their performance. The progressive reversion of their shares down to par value is a clear sign that they are expending their uniquely profitable opportunities, and no longer make a compelling case for further investment.

If the expected share price after profits are reported is less than $1, tax consideration of the individual shareholders may still lead him to take new shares rather than dividends, but otherwise he will always take the cash because he can always buy shares. If the corporation reported positive, but presumably disappointing, profits, the investor will have the cash. If they report a loss, he will get nothing and will see his holdings shrink by the extent of the loss. This is a very disagreeable outcome because he will see himself as being locked into an investment in a corporation that can not earn its cost of capital. The management can still draw investment by selling new shares in a secondary offering, and since they sell at a discount to par value the buyer has some assurance that the rate of return he will secure on his shares will not be less than, and will probably be more than, the corporation's internal rate of return. It would probably be a further reform in corporate governance to require shareholder approval for secondary offerings.

Unless the prospects of the corporation improve materially, it is right that capital be liquidated. If the problem lies in just a few losing operations, disinvestment will stop when they are closed or sold, and the price of shares will return to par value. Proceeds of asset sales are not of course included in profits, and are usually associated with recognition of losses.[5] The proceeds are therefore not available to the investors as dividends. It does not follow that corporation must retain the cash raised by asset sales. Far more desirable for everyone's point of view is for the management to repurchase shares when they are trading at a discount to imputed par value. "Imputed" par value in this context means the price at a point in time that is consistent with a price of exactly $1 after the next profit reporting date. The visibility of par value is just as important in this case as it was in guiding the decision to reinvest profits in a growing business. If the management is unwilling to impute values, they always have the option of simply waiting until the next reporting date.

Market Consequences

The implications for the stock market are profound and in my view beneficial. Note at the outset that it is not a logical necessity for there to be any impact on how the stock market behaves. If in fact the dividend payouts observed today were optimal and if the valuation of corporate assets and liabilities was to be left unchanged, the behavior of share prices would also be unaffected. I consider that outcome to be however extremely unlikely. The stock market would be profoundly changed, for the better.

How would share prices evolve under the rules that I propose? I will assume that dividends would be taxed as they are today. At the start of the first fiscal year of company X, its shares would be priced at $1. An investor knows two things with certainty: 1. a year out, he will have the option of forcing the management to honor its reported earnings in cash, and 2. to the extent that he foregoes this option he will have more or fewer shares depending on whether the company has profits or losses for the year. The price of shares can differ from unity during the year, depending on the expected difference between the rate of return of the company and the investor's alternative rates of return. This calculus suggests that investors make decisions on the basis of a rather short horizon. While that may seem contrary to the treatment of the future as presented in finance textbooks, it is entirely rational. It is moreover consistent with the empirical evidence, which is that the interest rate that is most highly correlated with market valuations is the year bill, and not the thirty-year bond.[6]

The payoff to the investor comes however not from price appreciation of a given position of shares, but from receiving more shares. That is a very big difference because the price of a share is set in a trading market—the stock market—while the reward of additional shares come directly from the management. It is not necessary to postulate that stock markets are very efficient, because their judgments of value are going to be checked at regular intervals. Not only is it going to be checked, it is going to be tested against a process in which the shareholders have a direct input by means of demanding the cash. As a result, the interest in the stock market as purely a trading vehicle—as markets for assets that are valued purely as trading opportunities—would be greatly reduced. Shareholders would not be forced to act like speculators, as they are today.

One does not have to go far to find an example of what this would mean in practice. It is widely—and in my view accurately—believed that in the late 1990's our stock markets were on an irrational bubble which shattered in September, 2000. Valuations were not justified by company fundamentals, as subsequent events demonstrated so painfully. In that greater fool market, it was always possible to suspend disbelief and instead to depend on dreams of greater wealth. The only winners in the end were the market makers, who book immense trading commissions while the public chased their dreams. Those same market makers have a perverse incentive to pump more hot air into the bubble because that generates volume and volume equals profits. It is a sobering fact—albeit perhaps the sort of truth that we are disinclined to credit these days—that Marx saw the terminus of capitalism as a state he called Financial Capitalism, in which the only people making money were stockbrokers.

It is always possible for greater fools to dream dreams of greater wealth than nature makes possible, and there is no way to prevent them from plunging into the stock market. The reality check that I am proposing is only intended to introduce more frequent reality checks and, along the way, to curb the manipulative powers of the market makers. I think the effects would be profound, but *caveat emptor* will always be a sound rule.

This should not be viewed as a frontal assault on Wall Street. Trading in shares would be greatly reduced, but it would be replaced in part—perhaps in large part—by underwritings of new, secondary offerings. The stock market could then perform the function for which it was created, which was to be a vehicle for raising equity capital. A corporation in need of investment could issue shares at par and sell them to investors, through the agency of the Wall street investment bankers. Only in today's distorted world has excessive retention of earnings replaced new issues.[7] Issuing of new shares in secondary offerings would almost surely be a far more frequent event, and the fees paid to Wall Street for that service would keep the wolf from their door. As the financial world presently operates, every effort is made—it seems—to avoid having to issue shares, and that is understandable. When the corporation exploits its shareholders, it is understandably hard to entice new ones to put in more money. But:

It is amazing to see how easy it would be to raise new equity capital by issuing shares when we treat the investors fairly.

184

In Today's Market

The ruinous taxation of corporate dividends, coupled with the practice of leaving it to the board of directors of the corporation to deny dividends to the investors, has made the stock market little better than a giant Ponzi scheme. The public and the scalpers alike buy shares in hopes of selling them later at a higher price. Few buyers—though this few includes Warren Buffet—expect to hold onto their positions long enough for dividends to matter. There are two results of this speculative myopia.

First, the corporation can confidently expect that essentially all earnings will automatically be reinvested in the business, and that they will never be required to account for even the most wasteful use of this capital.

Second, the buyers and sellers of the shares, since they expect to unload them rather quickly, have little incentive to do the due diligence on the operations and management of the company. They are understandably far more interested in how well the story will hold up.

These flaws in the stock market have visibly weakened it and distracted it from the task of efficient allocation of private capital. For several years now it has become apparent that stocks rise and stocks fall, but there is less and less hope that they are actually trending higher. The stock market has as a result become increasingly dependent on foreign investors. When foreign capital is flooding into our market, stocks rise and the dollar rallies in parallel. When foreign capital is exiting, the market and the dollar fall. This is not a reliable source of capital for corporate America. We need to stop the Ponzi scheme, and to make our markets more appealing to investors, even at the temporary cost of making less appealing to hot money traders.

Implementation

Any corporation can implement this plan unilaterally, subject to shareholder approval, and there are powerful incentives to do so. The method of implementation is simply to revise the corporate bylaws along the lines laid out above. I can see no reason why any corporation could not do this.

Would the shareholders want to adopt the proposed change in the bylaws? That is to ask, would they want to have the power to make the corporation recognize that it is the shareholders' money they are handling? I think that question answers itself, and it also answers the next question. Why would the corporation be willing to submit itself, its management, to the discipline of paying out all earnings to the investors? Because it is what the investors want. They would be far more willing to invest in such a management and would attach a higher value to any given earnings stream as a result. Quite simply, shares of corporations that adopted this rule would sell at a premium to shares of other corporations because they are treating their investors fairly.

While the corporation and its shareholders can implement this rule at any time, and already have an incentive to do so, they can not unilaterally amend the Internal Revenue code to correct the excessive taxation of dividends. To get the full benefit of treating investors fairly, it would eventually be necessary to reform the treatment of dividends, because at present the new shares that would be distributed would be treated as a dividend, and taxed immediately. If shareholders increasingly demanded that corporate America treat them fairly, there would also be a growing groundswell for reforming the tax code. In any case however, to repeat a point made earlier, a

186

very large part of domestic equity investment comes from sources which pay little or no taxes on dividends. Tax-exempt entities are just that. Accumulated assets of private and public pension funds likewise pay no tax on dividends. Most important of all, private I.R.A. accounts also pay no tax on dividends, and thanks to the latest changes in the tax code, long term investors pay taxes at a significantly lower rate. Collectively, these sources of domestic investment in equities account for nearly all of domestic investment capital.

While even in today's world the lion's share of all equity capital entering our stock market has preferential treatment of dividend income, short term traders do not. Traders have a job to do and a contribution to make to the smooth functioning of our capital markets.[8] At the present time however, they are being in effect subsidized, and their financial interests—interests that are never far from their minds—are in conflict with the interests of investors. It is neither envy nor malice toward the trading community to propose a leveling of the playing field.

The Difference Between Accounting Earnings and Economic Profits

Everyone knows that profits are defined in two distinct ways: on an accrual basis and on a cash basis. For most seasoned, ongoing corporations the difference is not large in any year, but for new, growing ones it can be very significant. Thus it is urgently necessary to address this issue here because it has to do directly with a possible discrepancy between reported profits and actual cash available for dividends.

For an established corporation the gap between accrued profits and profits on a cash basis reflects acknowledged difference between the timing of the recognition of costs and revenues. When it incurs an expense item, GAAP rules generally force the corporation to recognize the whole expense even though the actual outlays maybe distributed over a period of years. Similarly, when it contracts for future sales or services revenues, GAAP rules generally direct the corporation to book the revenues immediately even though the actual cash inflows will be distributed over a period of years. For existing corporations, GAAP earnings correspond to the revenues and costs recognized by GAAP accounting rules. Cash profits are, by contrast, based on actual cash flows as they occur in real time.

There is every reason why the corporation, when it reports profits, should report profits on both bases. That would permit the shareholders to form their reinvestment decisions in light of the actual current internal cash flows of the corporation, as well as the GAAP profit report. In practice, except for the treatment of post-retirement employee benefits, for an established corporation it is rare for the gap between accrued and cash profits to be very large. It is nonetheless entirely legitimate in principle to let the shareholders see directly the cash flow implications of the dividend claims; to see directly when the cash flow of the corporation might not be sufficient to cover dividend payouts.

One category of gaps between cash and accrual profits however is not addressed adequately at the present time, and would therefore demand some modification of accounting practices. I will take the case of a new startup corporation, although this issue can arise to some degree for any corporation. The issue has to do with the expensing of what are in reality investments.

Many of the outlays of young corporations are actually investments in their future. Advertising outlays provide a good example. Some of the benefits of advertising are realized immediately in terms of higher sales, but another portion is an investment in the franchise of the business. The size of this investment component—the exercise in building a recognized name and reputation—has been studied extensively in marketing research. I will not try to summarize it here except to point out that it is substantial, and it is a large part of why the corporation expects to grow in the future. There are many other examples. For the computer software companies, every problem surmounted by new computer code forms a platform from which to attack new problems, and solidifies the software library as a standard for applications by third parties. For makers of computer chips, every enhanced chip design is similarly the platform for further developments and future sales. Computer companies grow because of this follow-on reward from immediate developments. Computer companies—hardware and software—grow in much the same way that weeds invade a garden or bacteria invade a Petri dish: by getting a toe hold and growing it by the law of mass action.

There is no magic—there is no sure thing—in this process. The investment asset created in this way is a very risky creation that can evaporate without warning. There is no guarantee that any investment in advertising will actually build a valuable franchise. The competition is also advertising, and not everyone is going to win. Similarly, for computer companies, no amount of investment in computer code or a family of proprietary chips will guarantee success for that family. The competition are also expanding the range of their product families, and again, not everyone is going to win. It would not be entirely unreasonable for GAAP accounting rules to expense these outlays, even though the management intended them as profitable investments bearing rich deferred rewards.[9]

It is beyond my competence to judge whether, or how, to recognize deferred investment of this sort, but experts in accounting have had vast experience tackling that kind of task. The most extreme case is the one presented by a small but promising start-up, that will not have any positive net cash flow for years at best. These are companies that will need years to have put in place products and markets broad enough to provide for positive net cash flow. In the meantime, they report accounting losses, and certainly constitute the most pressing cases of the gap between true economic profits—which properly recognize investments—and cash profits. It is reassuring that they do not present an important problem for Redefining Shares. A simple, concrete example makes this clear.

Suppose start-up X Corp is ready to go public, and issues shares at $1 per value. Mr. A buys 10,000 shares for $10,000. Subsequently, X Corp reports losses every year. Mr. A gets no offer of cash, but instead suffers a steady dissipation of his holdings. This can end in either of two ways. Either the losses stop before they total $10,000, or X Corp loses the whole thing. If they lose all his money, A is simply wiped out and the very visible sign of it is that he has literally no shares left. If on the other hand X Corp eventually turns its business around, A has some shares left and X has some perhaps modest profits per share to report. In any case, the outcome is precisely the right one. The history of X's success or failure and the history of A's success or failure are identical. It is not the purpose of Redefining Shares to make X Corp a success or to make A rich. The more modest purpose is to ensure that they succeed or fail together. It is to avoid the situation where X's management is succeeding while A is failing.

Evidence from Privately Held Corporations

The dividend yield of publicly traded corporations has fallen precipitously over the last fifty years. This is actually a world-wide phenomenon, not limited to our corporate sector. The dividend yield of the S&P500 universe is now about 1 1/2%, but in 1950 it was above 5%. The dividend yield of the technology companies is virtually zero.[10] The natural inference from this history is that investors do not want dividends, but that is by no means the case. The vast majority of all taxable corporate entities in America are small, privately held corporations which have no publicly traded shares. These corporations are moreover more profitable than the publicly traded brethren—a fact that serves to confirm Gardiner Means' misgivings about the giant corporations. Dividend decisions at the closely held corporations are made by the owners, who have the authority to simply declare dividends to themselves at any time. Thus they should reflect very accurately the preferences of capitalists for cash dividends. What the historical record shows—as presented in the chart below—is that the pay out rate for all corporate America is high—nearly 60% of reported profits—and has actually been rising. In 1950, publicly traded corporations and privately held corporations both paid out about 40% of profits. Their practices have diverged significantly.

When the corporation is accountable to its owners, it serves their interests, meaning that it views cor-

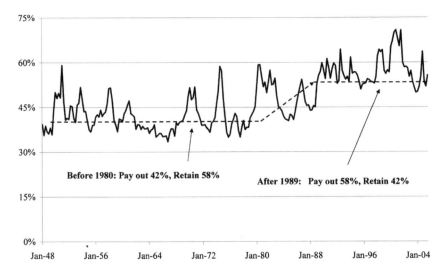

Payout Rate:
All American Corporations

Before 1980: Pay out 42%, Retain 58%

After 1989: Pay out 58%, Retain 42%

Source: Federal Reserve Board and Logistic Research & Trading Co.

porate earnings as their earnings. When it is not accountable to remote investors, it disregards their
interests. It is attentive instead to two other parties: the professional management and Wall Street.

Conclusion

The two salient facts that I cited previously, having
to do with clear evidence that managements retain too
much earnings, is unmistakable evidence that the stock
market is not efficient, and that more specifically, management has the capacity to manipulate investor information and investor opinion. Since in fact the

192

management of any business has unique access to crucial data, there is no perfect remedial action possible. The accounting profession tackles this imbalance and fights the good fight down in the trenches. Despite their best efforts however, it is manifestly evident that investors operate at a disadvantage in terms of vital information, and they operate under a further handicap, which is that they have—both individually and collectively—almost no way to make their voices heard in the management suite.

It is perhaps beguiling to think that there could be an effective collective approach to this inequality, and that is precisely what shareholder voting is supposed to achieve. But proxy voting has been almost totally ineffectual, as shown by studies that compare the success of firms with very dispersed ownership against firms with very concentrated ownership. A better idea is to empower the individual to act on his own behalf, without needing to engage in some costly and probably impossible group process. Let the investors decide what to do with their money.

Notes

1. The computer and computer software businesses are very susceptible to this kind of fraud because they invest in assets—their native software especially—which can depreciate very rapidly. In the presence of tight competition, no software innovation is safe from competition for long. Yesterday's proprietary breakthrough quickly becomes today's standard add-on.
2. The evidence is in this form: if one buys shares at a point in time, after a relatively few years his profit is dominated by the value of dividends received. Over a long holding period, dividends account for nearly all the profit.
3. They have of course an economic cost which equals the foregone dividend. Since however the dividend is fully taxable, the distribution of shares must also be fully taxable when they are sold.
4. It is very possible that the actual earnings report could cause investors to revise their expectations for future rates of return, and that the ac-

tual post-report price per share would be different from the one implied by the pre-report premium.

5. The corporation needs to clean up its accumulated losses when it exits ventures to the extent that it had previously failed to recognize losses as they actually occurred. That is to say, it will have an unreported loss to confess to if it had previously overreported profits. That will often happen innocently, because the management was not aware of how badly they were faring. To the extent that it reflects a policy to hide poor performance however, at least the investors had a chance along the way to call the management on its claims of profitability. They had a chance to take the cash at any time.

6. Every reader has been treated many times to the deep and passionate defense of "taking the long view," and there is indeed a place for that, but in managing a long term asset it is highly advisable to respect the so-called "Myopic Rule." It advises that in an uncertain world, the best way to maximize long term value is to revisit decisions frequently and to revise and adjust them as often as conditions change. It is called the Myopic Rule because it implies that at a point in time the agent makes commitments to maximize value only out to the shortest horizon possible.

7. At the present time, corporations generally issue new shares through the convertible bond and convertible preferred market, which is yet another anomaly. Why it is that a simple act like issuing shares should be wrapped in the mystery of complex and interacting embedded options is indeed hard to explain. The practice is usually explained as creating a kind of high dividend shares—the convertibles—or equivalently, as creating low coupon debt. Presumably the investor is befuddled by the embedded options into overvaluing the convertibles. While an explanation, it is hard to treat this as a justification.

8. Toward the end of full disclosure, the author freely admits to having been for many years a trader, and to having a deep and abiding affection, bordering on admiration, for his colleagues.

9. This was the problem of Digital Equipment Corp. They did not stint when it came to investing in their computer hardware and software, but when the time came to harvest the rewards, the competition had stolen the market from them. They invested, but they invested in ways that depreciated almost as fast as the money was spent.

10. The massive one-time pay out from Microsoft Corp, which was very well received by investors, is a striking exception, but one not repeated since.

15
Unemployment and Blame

Seventy years ago a contented and prosperous America leapt into a crisis that was shaking Europe from the Atlantic to the Urals. Across that entire European expanse—a land equal in area to America and of course far larger in population—feudalism was dying, and the vicious Isms of the twentieth century were presiding at the wake. Among them, only one seemed a true threat: Bolshevism and Bolshevik Russia. History, and the excesses of the Federal Reserve Bank in America, had conferred on Franklin Roosevelt the opportunity he needed to mobilize the nation for war against these enemies. He seized the chance, and proceeded under the banner of the New Deal.

The degree of mobilization that he needed—to mobilize all the resources of a very contented and reluctant nation that had shaken the dust of European wars from its boots—was completely unprecedented. It required that the federal government take on itself many of the powers and many of the self-proclaimed duties of the very regimes that it proposed to fight. Franklin Roosevelt became the functional equivalent of a Socialist dictator. In the crisis environment of the 1930's and 40's this was not hard to justify. As the crisis eased, with the death of German Naziism and Italian and Japanese fascism, moreover, the federal government was able to relax its grip. The return of peace in America—a gradual process of relaxation that started in 1945 but did not reach its conclusion until 1990—brought with it a return of the sorts of freedom that Americans were accustomed to. Indeed, what Americans call our Freedom are in fact not freedom as such, but are the fruits of Peace.

The Employment Promise

To rally a reluctant nation, the New Deal laid out a list of promises: guarantees that the federal government would make to the people. The guarantee of full employment was perhaps the central one of these. It goes without saying that it played well to a country that had endured a decade of hard times. The fact that those conditions had actually been caused by the federal government—first by the Federal Reserve and then by the costs of military mobilization—seemed not to matter, or perhaps not be understood.

Every crisis however leaves its scars. The deepest and costliest scar left by the New Deal was the promise of full employment. After that time, employment has been treated as a responsibility of the federal government. There is in fact nothing that they can do to raise the level of employment for any extended period of time. Even more to the point, there is nothing that the feds can do to raise the per capita real wage income for any extended period of time. Even if they could "create jobs" by forcing job sharing, it would not result in higher real wages paid, as the French have discovered.

Political Dynamite

The promise of full employment has thus become a political albatross. It is a promise that once made can not be revoked, but which at the same time can never be delivered! It is therefore a formula for perpetual failure. Every new administration goes down to Washington—or more likely, arises from the shadows in Washington—with the knowledge that it will fail to deliver on this promise. There are occasional bouts of relief, as with the Reagan administration that had the good fortune to preside over the end of the Depression of 1980, but only a fool would expect to be so lucky.

Every administration must, rationally, expect to fail to deliver on one of the most vital guarantees that it has inherited from the New Deal. I consider this to be a great danger to our political institutions. By taking on a responsibility that can never be met with any consistency, the federal government has guaranteed that the political discourse must be progressively divorced from the reality of failure.

A fellow who had spent the first half century of his life as a stolid Soviet citizen, residing in Tashkent, once described to me how the Soviet party propaganda mill handled the persistent failures of their regime. Each spring, he said, high level functionaries would appear on the television to address what went wrong last year and how everything was going to be better this year. The only problem was that matters never got better in any year. They actually got worse. Our employment situation has not gotten worse, because of the powerful productivity of our economy, but if employment should appear to lag behind the demands of the political pundits and our version of the propaganda line ensues: "We have to get this country moving again," "I have a plan," and so on. Whoever is speaking again does NOT have to get this country moving again; it is a self-starter, and on the other hand, he or she does NOT have a plan.

Make Work

In a previous chapter I presented the startling news about how many middle-aged men in America do not have work. They are not classified as unemployed because they do not claim to be looking for work—most probably find a little paying work in the grey economy of unreported jobs—but they are in truth unemployed. The powers that be, and which claim responsibility for our well-being and our livelihoods, can not help them to find work. Along with the millions—estimated at seven million—Americans who languish in prisons and jail, we have more than eleven million Americans who do not have work. Yet, according to the reckoning of the president of the country, they are "making" jobs all the time.

Who are they making jobs for, and what kind of jobs are they making? Library aide? Teacher's aide? Who is the government delivering its promise of jobs to? To the inner city? To Detroit, or Flint, or any one of dozens of other rust belt cities? Two categories of jobs have been on hiring binge for the last decade.[1] One is construction and the other is state and local government. The jobs in construction are real, but they barely offset losses in other blue collar fields. A recent study from the Department of Labor shows that it has not been natives but poor immigrants who have filled these jobs. Total employment in traditionally men's work has not grown. That leaves state and local government. It is easy to "make jobs" in state

and local government, because they are command economies. But is making jobs the same as making work?

**Make Work is not making Work, it is making labor.
Real Work makes itself, because it justifies itself by
what it accomplishes.**

The trade deficit, the failing to keep pace with new
technologies, the spread of the universal welfare subsidy
are all telling us that we need to make fewer jobs, but to
do more work.

Note

1. Based on data from the Department of Labor.

16

Do Not Confuse Effort Expended with Results Obtained

One of the most common mistakes in planning and in managing a task is to confuse the effort expended with the results obtained: to think of effort as being synonymous with results. We know how many hours the teacher spends with her pupils each day, and so we assume that they are learning; we know how many hours the scholar spends in his library and so we assume that he is gaining understanding. How do they say it? "Would that it were so." It is nonetheless amazingly easy to forget this rather fundamental fact, and we have Peter Drucker to thank for having pointed it out.

This note deals with two cases that highlight the difference between effort and results. Specifically, they deal with rethinking very practical management problems in which this confusion is so common. We need to stop thinking about what the functions are and who does what and redirect our gaze toward what is the outcome that is intended and how best to achieve it. The two cases are, first, a problem in highway repair, and second, a problem in maintaining a fleet of service vehicles. We will not trouble the patient scholar further, but will continue to assume that he is gaining understanding.

Road Maintenance

One of the inevitable prices exacted for modern civilization is that they have to repair all the roads every summer. In rough outline the job is very simple to describe, consisting of removing old pavement and old bridges and other structures, and replacing them with new ones. This summary does not however identify the desired results. Quite the contrary, it only describes the process, and in effect describes the inputs to the task: i.e. the effort expended.

The desired result is to restore deteriorated roads to service. It is the Roads, not the Repairs, that are the services being provided and therefore that are the desired results. At this stage all of this probably seems like nothing but a rather arid bit of hairsplitting. The crews that repair the roads are serving the purpose of making the roads serviceable. There will be no usable roads without their efforts. We pay them for their work. What is so complicated?

I will take as a given that the amount of miles of roads repaired per unit of time depends only on the amount of effort being expended. By making this assumption, I remove from consideration any questions relating to how hard or how dutifully the repair crews work, to whether they are properly motivated or supervised, or any other matter this could intervene between a simple headcount of the crews and the miles of road that they repair. That is, the effort depends upon the number of repair crews at work and thus is simply proportional to the expenditure on repairs. That is however not true of the results obtained. A given effort level can produce a wide range of results, depending on how it is employed.

It is in the nature of through streets and roads that

the amount of traffic that can pass along them is limited by the narrowest point, the most inhibited point on the whole stretch of road. Similarly, to limit the usable lanes of a bridge bottles up traffic on the roads that feed the bridge, and the congestion stretches far in every direction. The reason for repairing, and perhaps widening, the bridge is to facilitate traffic on all those roads. Now, unless the bridge was dangerously near collapse, traffic was crossing normally until the road crew showed up with their barriers and started to close lanes. The same is true of the roadway. Unless the potholes were mammoth, it provided adequate service to the traffic. This is not to say that the repairs should not be done, but it is the repairs themselves that in the short run cause traffic congestion and that represent the loss of service.

To provide the greatest results it is advisable therefore to minimize the disruption of traffic caused by the repairs themselves. To do that, it matters a great deal how the available crews are assigned. In general, the rule should be to assign all the available crews to work on projects one at a time. The disruption is nearly the same if one five-man crew is working on stretch of highway or if ten crews of five each are working on it. Ten crews however will finish the work in one-tenth the time, and return the road to service in one tenth the time. The "cost" is that during that time nine other highways are not being worked on, but that is hardly a cost at all. While the surface may be somewhat deteriorated, traffic still flows freely.

Taking the purely hypothetical numbers from the preceding paragraph somewhat seriously—not a serious proposal but a starting point—assigning ten crews to a single project until it is finished rather than spreading them among ten projects increases the flow of results by a factor of ten! Ten times as many roads are repaired and returned to service in any given period of time.

There are clear limits to bunching the efforts of the crews. Each crew has to gather in the morning and move out to its worksite. If the decisions are being made for a whole state, some of them may live hundreds of miles from the next site, in which case they would spend the whole day simply getting to work and back. In urban areas however—and that is where the lion's share of the work is located because of the intensity of wear—probably half the total crews available could get to almost any work site with about equal ease. There is no obvious rationale to be working on more than a few sites at a time across the whole metropolitan area.

Vehicle Fleet Repairs

My other example is for a repair shop that maintains a fleet of vehicles. As was the case with the road repairs, it is quite easy to identify the effort that is being expended. In this case it is the number of service bays that are busy at an given time. If we could imagine a homogeneous measure of "vehicle repair," an index that averages brake jobs and oil changes with repainting and tire balancing, then we could use that as the basis for a measure of effort expended. It is emblematic of the confusion of effort and results that the amount of "vehicle repair" done per unit of time is commonly thought to be a measure of results, but it is not. It is a measure of effort.

If the amount of repairs being done is not a measure of results, then how do we measure results? Indeed, what are the results? To answer that question it is only necessary to remind ourselves of why we have the repair shop and of why we have the fleet at all. It is not the repairs that serve the needs of the employees who use the fleet vehicles. It is the vehicles that serve their needs. The repairs are a necessary fact of life, but they are not in themselves an indication of the service that the fleet performs.

Since it is the vehicles in service that are the goal, the result of repairs is to put them back on the street, and the measure of results is how many repaired vehicles are put back on the road in a unit of time. I will assume that the effort being expended is put to good use: that the repairmen are not on coffee break half the day. Still, the results from a given effort can differ enormously, depending on the rules which direct that effort. The least productive rule is to work on the interesting cases: the vehicles that need the most extensive repairs. Suppose that there is a fairly steady flow of vehicles that need relatively minor work, and that the most difficult cases take six times as much effort as the simplest ones. Over the course of the time that one hard case can be returned to service, the same effort could have put six easy cases back on the road. If the repair shop spends half of its effort on the hardest cases and the other half on the easiest ones, it is returning seven vehicles to the fleet in the time that it could return twelve.

The rule of always finishing the hardest cases before working on the easiest ones is rather extreme, but it does not improve matters a great deal if the shop adopts a rule of always taking the next vehicle in line and working on it until it is finished. Every hard job that the mechanics tackle reduces by five (six minus one) the number of vehicles that they will return to the fleet in the time it takes to finish the hard job. The rule that maximizes the results is obviously to go to work immediately on all the routine maintenance jobs as they come in, even if that means leaving the more difficult jobs temporarily unfinished. Some refinements are needed to this rule, because if the set-up cost of stopping the big job, and then restarting it, is too large it would be better to finish it up. Recognizing this point would not, in my estimation, make a big difference in how the repair shop actually worked because it is rare that those set-up costs would be large enough to change the decision.

Analysis of the Cases

The two cases were discussed in rather simplistic, qualitative terms. To gain further direct experience of their implications it is necessary to work through some fact situations that apply them in more concrete settings.

Road Repair

Facts:

A given city has to resurface twenty major truck roads. Because they are thoroughfares, the cars and trucks that use them are almost entirely through traffic. What this means is that they stay on the road for several miles before exiting. For simplicity, I will simply assume that each of them is four miles in length, and that all traffic gets on at one end and continues to the other end. As a result, a disruption anywhere along a road adds greatly to the transit time of every vehicle that uses that road.

The city employs ten road crews, each of which is a team of six who always work together. These are highly proficient teams able to resurface one-tenth of a mile of road in a day. I will assume also that although these highways all need to be repaired, that they are serviceable in the short run in their initial condition.

Questions:

1. How many crew days are needed to resurface all the highways?

2. From the time that a crew starts to work on a given highway, how long does it take to complete the resurfacing if A. one crew does the whole job, B. two crews do the job, C. five crews work on that roadway, and D. all twenty crews work on it?

3. How many roads are under repair at a given time if A. each roadway is resurfaced by a single crew, B. two crews work simultaneously on a roadway, C. five crews work simultaneously on a roadway, and D. all twenty crews work at the same time on a single roadway?

4. If the disruption caused by road repairs is valued at $150,000 per day for each road that is being worked on, what is the cost per day of traffic disruption if One, Two, Five, or all Twenty crews work on a given roadway at the same time?

5. In total, how many days does it take for the ten crews to resurface all the roads? Is this a measure of results or of effort? Does it matter how crews are assigned to roads: either individually or by twos or by fives or all to the same road?

6. Assuming that all the crews can get to all worksites with equal difficulty, how would you propose to assign the work if you were managing the repair department?

Fleet Maintenance

Facts:

The county owns a repair shop for its vehicles which has six service bays and six mechanics. Cars and trucks are brought in between 7:30 and 8 a.m.; the mechanics start to work at 8. The vehicles line up in the order in which they arrive. The types of repairs needed can be grouped into three categories: major repairs, that will take two days to complete, moderate repairs that can be completed in a half day, and light maintenance that take an hour. The line consists of four major jobs, ten moderate ones, and forty light jobs. Assume that the actual order in which they line up is as follows: M, 5L, 2O, 5L, M, 5L, 3O, 5L, M, 5L, 2O, 5L, M, 5L, 3O, 5L. "M" denotes major, "O" denotes moderate, and "L" denotes light. The way to read this sequence is that the first vehicle in line is a major job, the next five are light jobs, then two moderate jobs, and so on.

We will consider three different work rules. Rule A is always to work on the hardest, and most interesting, job available. Rule B is to work on the next job in line, and rule C is always to work on the easiest job available.

The questions are based on timing the completion of the jobs. For each of the three rules, you will need to actually develop the completion schedule by hour. That is to say, how many vehicles are done after one hour, how many are done in the second hour, how many are done in the third hour, and so on until all the work is done. I will call this list a completion schedule.

Questions:

1. How many days will it take to complete all the work?

2. List the three completion schedules.

3. Compute the mean completion time under each rule. The mean completion time is the weighted average of the various completion times multiplied by the number of vehicles that are released at the end of that many hours. This sum is then divided by the total number of vehicles. An example follows:

Suppose that in a different repair shop, 3 vehicles are released after one hour, none are released at the end of two hours, 4 are released after three hours, and two are released after five hours. Then, the mean completion time is:

[3 vehicles X 1 hour + 4 vehicles X 3 hours + 2 vehicles X 5 hours] / [9 vehicles].

[3 X 1 + 4 X 3 + 2 X 5] / [3 + 4 + 2] = 25 / 9 = 2.78 hrs = 2 hrs 45 min approximately.

4. How does the number of days needed to repair all the vehicles differ between the three rules?

5. Which rule gets more results?

6. I rest my case.

Every measure of national income or product—e.g. Gross Domestic Product—is a measure of Effort Expended. There is no known national measure of Results Obtained.

17

Risk Management in the Wholesale Power Market: The California Energy Crisis

The electric power industry has been marred by a record of crises and business failures. Now FERC has presented a bold blueprint for the future which will promote transparency and restrain risk, but it is no panacea. Risk management will be a permanent feature of management of power providers and power users. We can draw some conclusions about costs and benefits of a risk management program from available data on the power markets.

In this essay we intend to explain the results of our historical study of wholesale power markets. Two questions in particular come to the fore: how would power options have performed in history, and what can we say about the tails of the distribution of spot prices. We will focus especially on those questions. This essay has been extracted from a much broader study of trading in electric power. Copies of the entire piece are available on request.[1]

Since deregulation of electric utilities and power transmission became a reality on a wide scale, the industry and consumers have had to cope with periodic crises in which the cost of power has risen explosively for brief periods of time. There are examples, probably familiar—not to say painfully familiar—to most persons who work in the industry, in which the spot price of power temporarily reached levels of ten or even a hundred times the usual cost of base load power. These crises were not merely expensive in dollars. During the height of each one, essential pricing relationships between subregions failed, the physical availability of power became problematic, and consequently the risks that producers and consumers were confronting were too great even to quantify. In brief, crisis became panic. The resulting price histories exhibit in many ways the behavior of financial markets when panic sets in. The methods of modern finance which have been developed to get people through financial crises are also applicable to power, as we will endeavor to explain here. We need however to pay attention to the actual causes of crises, because they influence the flow of events. Unlike financial crises, power crises have their roots in the physical realities of the production and delivery of watt-hours of power. The techniques of modern finance have a great deal to contribute to risk management but to apply them successfully requires that they be applied in the unique context of electric power.

At almost any place in the chain that starts with fuel acquisition and ends at the wall outlet there is potential for disruption. In practice however, as we will illustrate, the chief villain has been failure of the interregional transmission grid. Everyone in the utility industry is familiar with Transmission Line Load Relief orders. The aggregate statistics on the frequency are disturbing. The various subregions differ widely in the incidence of these TLR's. Taking the year 2000 and 2001, the subregion containing Cinergy, EMSC, reported 652 load reliefs. Main, which includes the city of Chicago, reported 773 relief orders. A simple aggregate count like this obscures important differences in severity, but nonetheless it is hard to ignore a record that amounts to more than one each day! In many subregions the physical facilities needed to maintain the integrity of the power grid appear to be less than satisfactory. FERC has wisely addressed this topic in its proposed rulemaking.

The root of the problem is that the major utilities that are responsible for providing interconnection have simply underinvested in this vital resource. The strength of the FERC rules is to create a free market in transmission and interconnection services so that the law of competitive supply can elicit adequate investment. As the new rulemaking takes effect and reshapes the industry, the crises should become less common and less severe. We can of course only look ahead to that world in a limited way because we are largely confined to rethinking the past and its data. With this proviso and its implication that any analysis needs constant updating to maintain its relevance and accuracy, we can begin.[2]

Crisis and Panic

When we look a little closely at what actually transpires in a crisis we gain some important insight into both the cause and the dynamics of wholesale power prices. We will not delve into a broad discussion of power crises here because there is only one key point that we need to observe. In normal times, prices of power between neighboring subregions are highly correlated. We will use the pair consisting of SP15 and Palo Verde: Southern California and Arizona, respectively. We take this example, because unlike the interconnection between northern California

Scatter Plot:
Same Day Spot Price of Wholesale Power

Source: Power Markets Week and Logistic Research & Trading Co.

and Mid Columbia, this particular interface was not considered to be a cause of problems or crises. In normal times the price basis between them is almost negligible, and it is clear that they inhabit a single market for wholesale power. In a crisis, not only are prices high, but they are only loosely correlated between subregions. We will illustrate these propositions with two graphs. The first one, above, shows daily price pairs in SP15 and Palo Verde over the period from March 15, 1999 to April 30, 2002.[3]

Most of the time, the price of wholesale power was less than $35 in both subregions and was nearly equal between them. As we move to the right within this chart however the relationship between the two price series at-

Scatter Plot: Outliers

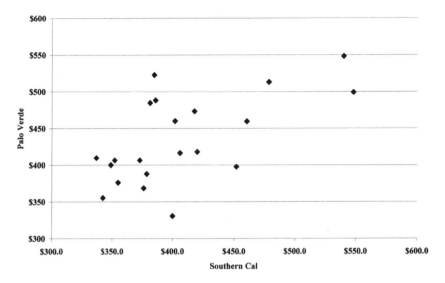

tenuates. The loss of correlation may not show as clearly as it should in this chart, because the dominant regime of high correlation trains the naked eye to see correlation. When we extract just those days of extreme prices—the upper right hand portion of this graph—the loss of correlation becomes more obvious.

The correlation of wholesale price for these crisis days is not zero of course. It is about 50%, as contrasted with a correlation of essentially 100% for the full sample. Nonetheless, the pure randomness of the individual prices—their capacity to change independently of each other—contributes not only to the Crisis, but to a deeper sense of Panic because familiar relationships that decision makers rely on daily no longer seem to be reliable at all. Crisis is the event that demands prompt and decisive

213

action, but panic is the condition that makes decisiveness very difficult to achieve.

There is one clear culprit behind a breakdown of the price correlation between subregions, and that is congestion or outright failure of the interconnect grid that joins them. Here again we are brought to the point that the FERC rulemaking addresses: the need to invest in the grid.

This history has important implications for risk management. First of all, it points clearly to an area of pressing need of risk control. FERC and utility management address the full range of risk control measures, but that is much too broad an agenda for our purposes. We need only to draw one inference, which is that in a crisis, prices become chaotic. It is difficult if not impossible at that time to make rational decisions regarding prices and trading decisions. The sorry example of the State of California, which seems to have panicked and locked in very high rates well into the future, provides a graphic illustration of this. It does not pay to try to make trading decisions in a crisis. What are needed are sound risk control and risk measurement regimes that have been put in place beforehand. The chaotic nature of price introduces a further complication, which is that familiar and accepted statistical models cannot be applied blindly. Better statistical methods are needed. We will come back to this point later on.

Power Options and Forward Contracts

It is possible to purchase wholesale power for the coming month at a preset price negotiated between the buyer and the seller. The terms of the contract typically specify the amount of power to be delivered each day of the month and the price. In the case of a few subregions there exists the alternative of market-traded futures contracts. The advantage of a futures contract is that it removes counterpart risk: the purchaser and the seller each deal with the exchange—the Nynex Exchange in New York—rather than with each other. The exchange is liable to both. Otherwise there is no economically significant difference between these two types of arrangements. Forward contracting is useful for many purposes but it does not really serve the needs of risk management for any entity that expects ordinarily to provide for its own load. Sometimes the purchased power will be a welcome addition, but most of the time it will simply replace power that could have been produced more profitably in-house.

It is possible but expensive to purchase power one day ahead in the spot market. That freedom does directly tackle the needs of risk management for coping with some kinds of emergencies.[4] The management of a utility can for instance offset temporary curtailments of its own native generation in this way. For crises with wide impact on the spot price however, the daily spot market provides no control of price risk. It would be better and cheaper to purchase in advance, and for a fixed term, an option to take power any day at a predetermined price. Not only is the cost of purchased power known in advance, but the need for daily trading and negotiating are eliminated. Power options fill this need by giving the purchaser the right to buy up to a fixed amount of power on any day at a fixed price. Typically, the unit of time for power options is one month.

Risk management has two complementary parts. The role of power options is to contribute to risk control. Risk control—which is of course only partial control under the best of circumstances—consists of achieving a degree of operational control in the face of conditions that face the firm. Power options actually provide a high degree of management control over price spikes in the wholesale market. The one important qualification that must be made is that they are useful only when the interconnect grid is itself operational. Most financial options are settled, or can in effect be settled, in cash. Because an electric utility is required, to the degree possible, to deliver power on demand, electric power options must settle up in actual watts of power. The terms of the option cannot insure that this will be possible in a crisis. As a consequence, the FERC rulemaking will have the effect of making power options more useful to the degree that it makes the performance of the grid more reliable. Actually, not only is it true that power options have an important part to play in risk control, a stronger statement could be made. Control of price risk always amounts to replicating the behavior of options, either by actually purchasing options or by adopting trading discipline that replicates the behavior of option payoffs.

The other part of risk management is risk measurement, which consists of quantifying the cost of the hazards that confront the management of the business. The essence of risk is mystery; risk is what we do not know. Still it is possible to quantify the statistical distribution of potential losses by using actual past experience in combination with statistical methods and models. The nature of the price history of recent years and unavoidable features of power options, require that we rely less on conventional models and rely more on analysis of the data directly. All too often we find that quantification means in practice scaling the parameters of some pre-shrunk model. We do not by any means reject models where we think that they are likely to succeed and to provide valuable insight. They are not however the heart of our approach to risk measurement. Rather, our approach is to pose important questions which arise from the actual decisions that management needs to be prepared to make, and to apply the historical data directly to them. What this means in practice will become clearer as we address two central issues, both of which bear on the costs and benefits of power options.

The first question is this: What can we say about the process that describes the maximum price that will be observed in any given month? To what extent is the maximum predictable at the end of the preceding month—in time to purchase power options if that seems warranted—and what factors are leading indicators of the maximum? Given a best forecast of the maximum, moreover, what can we say about the statistical distribution of the actual maximum achieved in relation to the forecast.

The second question has to do directly with options. The value of options depends critically on the statistical properties of the process that generates prices over time. Because the statistical process that describes the price of wholesale power is so very chaotic, conventional models of option pricing cannot be applied. We can however compute the actual historical payoffs that would have been achieved by options. Each day the option payoff is either zero—in case the option is out of the money—or it is the difference between the actual price of wholesale power and the strike price of the option. Once we specify a rule that dictates the choice each month of an option strike, it is a simple chore to recreate the historical payoffs. The costs and benefits of power options can then be judged on the basis of how they would actually have performed, free of any dubious assumptions about stochastic processes.

Study of the Maximum Price

The business risk associated with price spikes is directly related to the highest price. Accordingly, no single bit of information is as useful as the distribution of the maximum price that can occur within the horizon of the decisions that must be made. We will simply take that horizon to be one month. What have we discovered about the statistical behavior of the maximum price?

Before we discuss the predictive model, it is instructive to summarize the behavior of the residuals—the unsystematic component of the maximum price—from a regression model of the maximum. The chart below illustrates the chaotic nature of price shocks. It is a histogram of the residuals from a simple regression in logarithms of the maximum price within a month. The right hand side variables are also logarithms; the log of the average price within the same month, the average price for the preceding month, and the maximum price for the preceding month. We chose these variables for this test because we want to understand the relationship that exists between the maximum that occurs in a month and the average price for the same month. It is not a predictive model of course, since it includes the average spot price within the month. Since the contemporaneous average price has, understandably, great explanatory power for the maximum, the fitted residuals from this regression model are as "tame" as they could be. The data that underlies this study consists of all months for which full data exists, covering all power subregions. There were 568 monthly observations in all, of which, for example, fifty-eight come from TVA and seventy-five come from the Mid Columbia subregion.

What the chart shows is that even when we use in-

Frequency

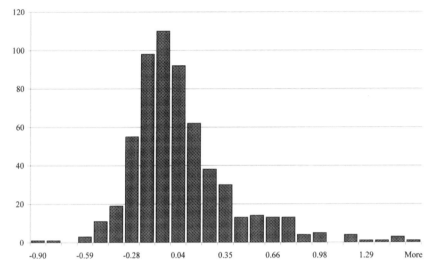

Source: Logistic Research & Trading Co.

formation about the average price in the same month, and even when we take logarithms of all the factors, the unexplained residuals are still highly positively skewed. What this means in practice can be made clear in a simple contrast. In twenty-eight of the months, out of a total of 568 months, the maximum price was two times the fitted value from the model. On the other hand there are no months in which the fitted value was two or more times the actual maximum price. These twenty-eight monthly observations are of course the twenty-eight most interesting—or most frighten-ing—months in the whole sample and yet even a model that controls for the average price each month would underpredict the maximum by 100%.

We do not propose to try to "correct" the data or the models for the skewness of the model residuals. Quite the contrary, this skewness—what we have elsewhere termed the chaotic nature of the price shocks—is real. In any given month, the markets sample from a positively skewed distribution like this one. It is entirely sufficient for purposes of risk management to have quantified the residual distribution, and especially to have an estimate of the degree of skewness. The significance of this distribution of residuals, for our purposes, is that it permits us to quantify the distribution, which is precisely the distribution of price shocks that occur in times of crisis. Residual distributions like this one, therefore, are an integral part of risk measurement.

The only way to deal with random innovations is through quantification of their stochastic properties. The maximum price is not entirely random however. A component of it can be anticipated before the month has begun, and this part—the systematic component—is both a useful management tool and a source of insight into the process that causes price shocks. Two further questions can be addressed to the available data. How significant is weather in causing price spikes, and are available price forecasts useful in predicting them. The power trading market provides the industry with forward contracting prices that are in the nature of forecasts of the average price to prevail of a given month in the future. It is an interesting question how good these forecasts are, and what is the source of their insight if any. We have looked at this issue.

Temperature

It is obvious that price shocks are to a large extent provoked by extremes of weather that generate an exceptional drain on the power grid. This is borne out in our data, when we add the average monthly temperature as an explanatory factor.[5] The average temperature makes a significant contribution to explaining the maximum price observed during the month.

Forward Prices

For the purposes of this study, we use the forward price quoted on the last day of the preceding month, which is of course the last day in which it is still purely a forecast. Since these prices should have the attributes of price forecasts, it is of some interest to see what light they shed on the maximum price. Several conclusions can be drawn. The available data on forward prices is unfortunately somewhat limited, and as a result we could investigate the relationship for only a subsample consisting of about 200 monthly observations.

The forward price contains useful information about the maximum price even when we hold constant other predictive factors like the average price and the maximum price in the preceding month. Evidently, energy traders possess some information that is not simply an extrapolation of the recent past. When we also hold constant the average price in the month—the average that the forward price is a forecast of—the forward price becomes insignificant. This suggests, reasonably enough, that whatever information is embedded in the forward price is information about the average price over a month, and that the forward has no additional insight specifically about the maximum price. It further strengthens our conviction that the magnitude of price spikes is in fact entirely random and unpredictable.

While the forward price adds useful information about future prices, it is not by any means an efficient forecast. That is to say, any forecast that uses the forward price can be improved upon by adding some other factors as well. The insight that they provide is not reflected in the forward price. One factor that the forward price does however anticipate is the mean temperature. In any model that contains the forward price of electricity, adding the mean temperature to the model does not add anything to it. As we mentioned previously, temperature is itself very much related to the maximum price. The point we are making here is that temperature adds nothing further to any model that controls for the forward price, and that is because the trading market is able to forecast the mean temperature pretty accurately.

These statistical models serve to identify that part of the maximum price than can be anticipated, and that serves as a best point forecast. They go part of the way to reducing or explaining the rather chaotic component of the maximum. Typically, a model of this sort explain between 50% and 60% of the variance in the logarithm of the maximum price. The skewed residuals remain, and as we have explained already they can parameterize their distribution as well.

This model documents the fact that the historical data—even data as unconventional as this—yields valuable information when we take off the blinders of predetermined models and put on the decision maker's spectacles, through which we pose question of the history. Following in this vein, there is another way to look at this data which, if anything, bears even more directly on hedging and risk management.

Valuing Call Options

As we observed above, the tools for managing price risks are largely an exercise in valuing options to cover the risk from outliers. In general, the contribution that quantitative research makes is two-fold: to calculate values of options and to formulate trading rules that replicate the outcomes of options. Conventional theory requires one to specify at the outset the kind of distribution that governs prices. The well-known Black-Scholes Model, for instance, starts with the assumption that the logarithm of price is normally distributed. As we know all too well, the price of wholesale power is far too erratic to succumb to any convenient model. Indeed, the times where management is *most* in need of reliable valuations are precisely those times when conventional models are the most inaccurate! As usual, we want to start not with assumptions, but with the history.

The behavior of prices that we discussed above shows clearly that conventional models do not apply to options on wholesale power. There is hardly any need to stress how much the distribution of price deviates from a normal distribution because of the random incidence of large spikes. There is another, equally important way in which familiar option models misrepresent this data. In finance theory, options are valued indirectly, by computing the payoff of a dynamic hedging strategy that replicates option outcomes. We assume that price evolves by some sort of random walk, in which the price tomorrow is related to the price today by the addition of some sort of increment—whether from a normal distribution or not—but wholesale power is anything but a random walk. It would be more accurate to say that each day is drawn from the same distribution as the previous day. The random walk assumption must be made in order to justify any hope of dynamic hedging. Random walk price paths have the property—essential for conventional option models—that all price changes are permanent, but the price spikes that occur in electric power, by contrast, are essentially transient phenomena. If dynamic hedging is not feasible, the Black-Scholes-Merton approach to modeling options is not valid. Under these circumstances, it is meaningless to propose any dynamic hedging method, and equally meaningless to attempt to value options by that method.[6]

Using the price data, we instead constructed the history of option payoffs, by sub-region and by month. The terms of the standard call option on wholesale power are very familiar: each single option entitles the bearer to draw one mega-watt-hour of power each day of the month at a predetermined strike price. Thus it is like a strip of daily options, one for each day of the month. The option payoffs are simply the realized value each month of such a compound option. There are many questions that we would want to pose, but perhaps the most central one is this: historically, have power options been more valuable in months where we would predict a high maximum price than in months where we would predict a normal maximum?

Does our forecast of the maximum price for a given month tell us anything in advance about how valuable the option contract will turn out to be?

The answer is a very resounding affirmative. Before

we can arrive at any numbers, we need to specify the terms of the contract. Specifically, we have to have some rule that chooses a strike price each month. In order to be sure that our results are not an accident of the way we make this choice, we tested various rules, but the simplest one is indicative of all. We tested a rule which fixed the option strike at a percentage spread over the expected average spot price for the coming month. Thus, for instance, if at the start of a month we forecast that the daily spot price would average $24, and if we fix the spread at 10%, then the option outcome consists that month of the realized value of an option to buy power at $26.40. As the expected spot price changes from month to month and from subregion to subregion, the dollar strike adjusts accordingly but the ten per cent spread rule remains the same.

The answer to the question posed above lies in the correlation between the realized value of call options and the expected maximum, as of the start of the month. It is not appropriate however to simply correlate them, because both are extremely skewed by those rare months of radical price spikes. To obtain a more reliable measure of the correlation, we made two adjustments: first of all, we related not the raw factors, but their logarithms. This reduces the importance of the few extreme months. Secondly, we added a constant to the option value each month, before calculating the logarithm. The exact value of the constant intercept is another statistic that we estimate. The model therefore takes the following form:

ln (Option Outcome + Constant) = A + B * ln (expected Maximum) + u.

We estimate the three parameters—A, B, and Constant—simultaneously. The estimated correlation is 50%, which has a t-ratio of 13.5. This correlation coefficient is somewhat inflated by price correlation across neighboring sub-regions means, because the data we use are not entirely independent observations. It is appropriate to adjust—to deflate—the t-ratio. Even if we take the conservative step of dividing the t-ratio in half, it is still extremely significant. The actual estimate of the Constant is $3.85, and the estimate of B is 68%. A one per cent increase in the expected maximum price adds about two-thirds of a per cent to the expected option outcome plus $3.85. An example may help to clarify this calculation. In October 1999, the expected maximum price—expected as of the end of September—was $46.35. The following month, the expected maximum had grown to $70.65. The expected value of an option contract of October therefore was:

Expected Option Value October = exp (−.73 + .68 * ln (46.35)) − $3.85 = $2.83.

The following month,

Expected Option Value November = exp (−.73 + .68 * ln ($70.65)) − $3.85 = $4.86.

The expected option value would be about $2.04 higher each day of November, because the expected maximum price was also higher in November.

Conclusion

Quantitative data can yield a rich harvest of information that adds value to business decisions, but in order to extract the information it is necessary to view the data as evidence and the study as an exercise in uncovering statistical evidence. This is the approach that we term the Stochastic approach. All too often studies begin with a commitment to force the data into one or another standard sort of model whose only virtue is that one would know how to interpret the results. When we start off with a particular sort of model it is nearly certain that the actual data will violate the assumptions that the model requires, and the results will actually be useless.

The place to start is with an understanding of the business problem at hand: What do we need to know, what sort of evidence and estimates would help us to make better decisions. No data and no model will make all the decisions. On the contrary, our only expectation is a more modest one, which is that the evidence we uncover will be of some value. The next step is to let the data speak for itself. Does it provide any basis for useful evidence or valuable estimates? What can it tell us that will make for better decisions?

This is the way we have approached the history of the price of electric power. Our study of this topic is of course by no means finished. It is continuing exercise in rethinking the questions we wish to pose and the methods that are most appropriate to address them. Even at this relatively early stage however we feel that what we have uncovered should be interesting to the utility industry and to power traders, and perhaps to regulators as well.

Notes

1. This study was completed in Spring, 2003. Fortunately the nation has been largely free of crises since then.
2. Our data comes from the Power Markets Week database.

3. The decision to purchase power must be made the previous day. This should actually smooth the reported price series.
4. The daily spot market does not solve all critical problems, because understandably it is necessary to purchase power that is needed for a given day some time on the preceding day. This limitation is unavoidable because it is intrinsic in the physical realities of power generation and transmission.
5. Temperature, for this purpose, is the average daily temperature in the largest metropolitan area within each subregion.
6. This statement is a bit oversimplified. Certainly, periods of high prices are grouped together because the causes—weather and the like—are somewhat persistent phenomena. Spikes however generally persist for only a few days, after which price drops precipitously.

Two Essays on the Financial and Commodity Markets

18

The Perfectly Inefficient Market

The theory of modern capital and risk markets has spawned a lively and highly informative investigation of the Perfectly Efficient Market. As important as are the insights that we derive from this inquiry and as valuable a tool as it is for research into the markets, it is increasingly clear that it does not actually describe financial markets at the present time. We need more tools, and toward this end I propose the Perfectly Inefficient Market hypothesis. Although this name may seem facetious, that is by no means the case. It is possible for a market in equilibrium to generate its own price variance in the absence of any information flow whatsoever. It is possible for a market to be perfectly inefficient, and that state once achieved would in fact be a stable equilibrium.

Inefficient Markets

There is no need to reproduce a lengthy account of the Efficient Market Hypothesis because that is available from many sources. Since however the Inefficient Market Hypothesis is in some ways defined in contrast to it, a brief summary of efficient markets is a good place to begin.

In an efficient market, prices are informative. A market is, in Fama's terminology, efficient to the extent that market prices reflect all the available information which logically bears on the values which are being traded in the market. In the case of the stock market the sorts of pertinent information are things that bear on the earnings and profitability of the listed corporations and facts that shed light on the equity risk premium. In the case of agricultural commodities, information about crop yields and weather are important information. Efficiency is a matter of degree and it is difficult to be any more specific than this. In its purest form however, we can specify what is perfect efficiency. A market is perfectly efficient when prices reflect all available information and nothing else. That is to say, every price change is the result of new information entering the market. There is no trading noise at all; given the current information set the supply and demand for the entities being traded are perfect elastic at the "Rational" price.

It is therefore easy to appreciate what is an inefficient market. It is one in which price changes are not entirely due to the arrival of new information. A market is inefficient to the extent that there is noise. A market is Perfectly Inefficient when there is *only* Trading noise: when the flow of arriving information has no correlation with price at all. This contemplates a special case in which there is in fact no information to arrive. If prices in such a catatonic market never varied at all, the market would by default be perfectly efficient. In reality there will always be some noise, whether there is any information or not. Any price variation would therefore be due in this special case entirely to noise, and the market would be perfectly inefficient. This observation by itself is not terribly interesting. As long as the magnitude and persistence of noise are damped by a market process and are in fact small and brief, inefficiency of this sort would be a sort of minor annoyance. I will endeavor to make the case that under very natural market conditions market forces may magnify rather than dampen the size and persistence of noise, and I will point out some of the features of markets at the present time that have that effect.

It has always been recognized that efficiency of any actual market is a matter of degree, lying somewhere between perfectly efficient and perfectly inefficient. Assessing the degree of efficiency is therefore an empirical chore which draws upon specific behavior of that market. There is little that one can say priori; this important topic must be left for the econometricians. We can however explore the special case of Perfect Inefficiency. As we do so, we will gain a better appreciation of how inefficiency works and why it happens, and of why markets are not perfectly efficient.

Bid—Ask Spread and Efficiency

Since the cause of inefficiency is the rational behavior of participants in a market, we can start the analysis by looking into the actions of market makers. There is a component of price which is generally accepted to be uninformative, and that is the bid—ask spread. Since the presence of a bid—ask spread is consistent with prices that are otherwise efficient, and since it exists because of the need to compensate market makers for their services, we do not ordinarily think of it as an inefficiency, but in principle it is. Transactions that take the price path back and forth across a bid—ask spread are price events that are not indicative of the arrival of information, and would not be found in a perfectly efficient market. More realistically, in an almost perfectly efficient market the bid—ask spread would be so small as to account for a negligible component of the total variance of price. It will serve us later on to invest some time here to think through the market makers' spread.

Consider, as the most elementary case, a market in which the equilibrium price does not change at all over time, and in which it is well known that it does not change. Imagine moreover that market makers are competitive price takers. There will be a spread between bid and ask because of the time cost of money and uncertainty about the flow of orders. Specifically, when an offer hits the market, market makers will bid somewhat below the equilibrium price because whoever winds up taking the offer will have to hold an inventory for some length of time. He is financing the party that came in to sell the asset. He has some uncertainty, moreover, that represents a significant component of his cost. At some indeterminate future time, other parties will arrive to buy the asset, but the market maker confronts two unknowns. He does not know how long he will have to hold his inventory before a buyer comes to the market, and he does not know if he will be the one to hit that bid when it does arrive. If another market maker fills the new bid, by shorting the asset, the long will have a choice either to wait for another buyer, or to sell to his colleague, the short, at some price between the bid and ask that they quote to the public. How large is the cost associated with this uncertainty depends on the size of the block that he initially took down. The larger it is, the longer he will have inventory and the more vulnerable he is to his colleagues.

This dynamic can be expanded upon to incorporate the effect of bunching of orders that enter the market. In practice orders are bunched both temporally and in magnitude. By temporal bunching I mean that intervals of time when the vast majority of orders are on one side or the other of the market. In the case of the stock market for instance, it is not unusual for retail supply or demand to dominate for as long as a week at a time. That is to say, it is not unusual for the vast majority of transactions to consist either of net sales to the public or net purchases from the public for an entire week running. Bunching in magnitude connotes the actual size of the net retail bid or ask over a period of time. The risk to a market maker of hitting a bid which leaves him short the asset is that not only will it be impossible for him to cover for a long time—understanding "long" to be measured in the highly myopic time scale of the trading world—but that subsequent buy orders will move the price increasingly far from the fixed equilibrium.

In the artificial framework we adopted here, in which the equilibrium price does not change and is known and agreed upon by market makers, the extent of bunching is constrained by the patience of retail supply and demand. The random incidence of non-informational trades will introduce some bunching. Bunching is especially prevalent when non-economic entities are present. What the public sees is a price path that exhibits persistent deviations from what is in fact the unchanging price equilibrium, because the market makers adjust to persistent order imbalance. It is highly likely, if not positively certain, that the public will endeavor to discern some deeper meaning in these price bubbles. As long however as the fixed equilibrium holds, one would expect the public to become more patient in the face of what they perceive to be largely transient, irrational price fluctuations. The willingness and ability of the public to wait, coupled with the capital base of the market makers will enforce a bound on the magnitude of deviations from equilibrium price, although non-informational trades are also generally driven by decisions with a high degree of urgency.

There is a force opposed to this one, however, exacerbating bubbles. The market maker has only one lever—his bid and ask—to rationalize two different risks—uncertainty about the price at which he will unwind the position he acquires and uncertainty about when he will unwind it. Specifically, the faster he wants to close out his position, the lower must his bid be, and the higher the ask. This is quite an intuitive proposition. If he is unwilling to hold an open position for very long and if he wants to enter the position at a price that provides a good chance of profit, he will have to widen his bid—ask. If he is buying, for instance, he will have to pay a small enough price that he is likely to sell higher within his short time frame. If he was more patient, on the other hand, he could bid more aggressively, confident that his price would be reached. This dynamic introduces the essential connection between risk and the bid—ask spread.

The more unwilling the market maker is to hold an open position, the less aggressively he will bid and the more aggressively he will offer.

To the degree that orders to buy and sell are unrelated to the arrival of information, the price path will be characterized by a volatile transitory component. The presence of this component has two effects, one direct and one indirect. The direct effect is to make market making a more risky venture and therefore to shorten the market maker's horizon. He will want to exit positions rapidly. The indirect consequence is therefore that he will widen his bid—ask spread. But at this turn there is a dangerous feedback, because it is the bid—ask spread that supports or causes the transitory component in the first place. Thus, the attempt of the individual market maker to restrain his risk makes this market less efficient, and forces all the other market makers to take similar action. The essential question that we want to investigate is whether inefficiency can be self-justifying, and whether it can actually be explosive.

A Model of Perfectly Inefficient Market

The model that follows is in the nature of a purely hypothetical model of a market. It could be any financial market, either a market for financial assets or a market for risk positions. The actual characteristics of the traded objects are not important. What is important is the constraints which bear on the players in the market. The objective of this exercise is to draw conclusions about how prices would evolve. I will simplify the analysis by assuming that there is in fact no relevant information whatever, but that there is an asynchronous flow of orders to buy and sell. There is always some valuable information entering a market, but as we will see subsequently, it may not pay to trade on it. In any case, at this juncture we wish to focus on the noise. I will moreover focus attention on a hypothetical market maker who is attempting to accommodate this flow. Our goal is to establish, in a general and theoretical way, that even as extreme a result as Perfect Inefficiency is possible.

While Perfect Inefficiency is possible, it is not at all normal or common. The normal state of affairs in any asset or risk market is some compromise between efficiency and inefficiency. It is only natural therefore that some unusual conditions must obtain to support Perfect Inefficiency, and I will have to appeal to them. To be specific, I will assume two facts about the retail order flow.

1. I will assume that a large component of orders are non-economic, in the sense that they are not motivated by profit-seeking motives.
2. I will further assume that many of the economic agents in the market—the market makers themselves and many of the "public" as well—are leveraged speculators. Note moreover that agents we think of as "investors" are for this purpose truly speculators: they are price takers who seek to profit from future price corrections.

Before proceeding it will be useful to define and explain these assumptions more fully.

Non-economic Agents

A non-economic agent is simply an entity that trades in the market for reasons unrelated to profit. The most noted example is the Federal Reserve Bank, through its Federal Open Market Committee. The Federal Reserve Bank is in fact an enormously profitable enterprise. It is in fact by far the single most profitable corporation in the world, but its profits do not come from its trading activities. They come from the seignorage profits that fall from its monopoly of the right to create cash dollars. It prints money, at essentially no cost to itself, and with this money it purchases assets that pay interest. The resulting interest flow is gigantic. In a recession, which is characterized by financial distress amongst financial institutions, it is not rare for the profits of the Federal Reserve to approach the combined profits of all other financial institutions.[1] The Fed's open market actions are not however gauged to enhance its profits. They reflect policy decisions that are motivated by the needs of member banks and ultimately by a view of the national interest.

At the present time there are many other non-economic agents, or agents with very mixed motives. The other two great central banks—the Bank of Japan and the Central Bank of Europe— are the largest of them. Many entities that hold large positions of common stock are also essentially non-economic. While our federal government does not own stocks, many foreign governments invest in our equity markets. The petro-dollar funds are immense, and so are entities like the Singaporean national retirement fund. While they surely prefer more investment returns to less returns, their decisions are swayed by, or even dictated by, political calculations. Political agents—those like the Fed that report directly to political governance—have their freedom constrained by the needs of their governors.

The Federal Reserve System in the United States has an established tradition of operational rules that make its policy decisions predictable to a degree, but that degree is not really very large. The extreme volatility of interest rates both before and after meetings of the Open Market Committee must dispel any notion that the markets are able to anticipate what action will be taken. Other government entities, both in America and abroad, are far less predictable. Their attitude seems to be that market makers and speculators are paid generously to take risk, and so that is what they should do, while governments do whatever is necessary to promote the national interest.

Leverage

Leverage forces agents who are otherwise models of economic acquisitiveness to make uneconomic trades of two kinds. Leveraged speculators take positions that, if they go wrong, can consume all the agent's capital in a very short time. For this reason, very few speculators survive for very long. We need not dwell on the mystery of why they keep trying. It is a fact of life.

When a speculator's position is going against him, he must be ready to close it out simply to avoid risk to his survival. This is far from easy to do, because most of the time he would have been better off, *ex post*, defying the fates and sticking to his position. He can not do that very often however because failure is a terminal state. He can win many showdowns with the odds, and generate a handsome income along the way, but he can only lose one. He has to recognize the necessity for stops.[2] On the other side, when a position is working, he has an analogous problem which is to know when to take a profit. It is an enticing option, one would think, simply hold onto any position that is working, but that is sure to lead to ruin, for reasons that are really quite obvious.

The speculator will exit any given position at some time. There can in theory be exceptional cases where a speculator has latched onto a position so profitable that he lets it run until the day he retires, but they are so infrequent as not to merit our attention. The speculator is going to close out his position. Now, there are only two possibilities: either he leaves with a profit or he leaves with a loss. If he never settles on a profit target, he is sure to exit on a stop. Now, he may still have a profit, because once he has accrued a profit he can place a stop behind himself at a point where he still has a profit even if his stop is hit, but a policy always to exit on stops is almost surely headed for disaster. Exiting only on stops is a virtual formula for losses. Even seasoned traders are heard to complain that "the only thing stops ever did for me was to stop me from making money."

There is a vast lore which purports to tell speculators where to take profits and where to set stops, but despite claims to the contrary it is not very effective. If it was, most speculators would survive and profit, whereas in reality most fail. In practice, stops are set at the point where a tolerable loss becomes intolerable. Limits—exit points on the favorable side[3]—are similarly set where some profit target is hit. The point is that stops and limits are almost entirely independent of any amount of information about the asset or the position that is being taken. They must necessarily be rigid rules that do not bend to developments in the market, because they are dictated not by trading judgments based on specific information, but by the business needs of the trader.

The combination of stop and limit orders creates a dynamic that is similar to and reinforces the bid—ask spread. Consider a speculator who has hit his stop and sold his long position. He still believes in the thesis that underlies his position; he still believes that the long position should be profitable. His problem is to know where to get back into the market. He stopped himself out because he feared that the risk of further decline had become intolerable. He is accordingly unlikely to get back in at a lower price. The fact that the price continues to fall reaffirms the wisdom of his stop. He is unlikely to get back in until the market has regained some upward momentum, as evidenced by breaking through the point where he was stopped out. The gap—the difference between his stop and the higher price where he reopens his position—is a pure cost of the stop and it is analogous to an adverse bid—ask spread. To sum up to this point, the speculator almost never buys at the bottom—it is too risky there—or sells at the top.

Putting It Together

The inefficiency of a market is pure risk. The greater the inefficiency that is present, the more risky it is to take positions in the market. Since however inefficiency does not enhance the expected gain from trading and investing, it is uncompensated risk.

This proposition should be self-evident. An efficient market is one in which risk is only the unavoidable risk associated with the flow of new information about the asset or position that is being traded. That is the smallest degree of risk that there could be. Inefficiency is risk, and it is very "pure" risk in the sense that there is no associated return.

A market is inefficient to the degree that little is known about the future of traded assets and risk positions, and in the extreme—in the Perfectly Inefficient Market—nothing is known about even the proximate future.

Consider a market that is hit at random times by orders from non-economic agents. These orders are furthermore generally large in relation to the market because the purest non-economic agents are very large institutions. Since these orders are placed by agents without regard to predictable economic factors and without regard to the cost of executing them, they hit like bolts out of the blue. Faced with an order of this sort, the market maker must still come up with a bid and ask. In doing so, his only source of information is the historical price distribution. It actually makes no difference that he knows that the equilibrium price has not actually changed, and that the order in hand is perfectly uninformative. Any trade in this market is by definition irrational; investors would simply not buy or sell assets or take risk positions in which there is no prospect of gain or loss. Since the order in hand is, therefore, inherently irrational it is difficult to know what is the rational response to it. Lord Keynes had a saying for cases like this: "Nothing is more irrational than a rational policy in an irrational world." The market maker does not have the option of surrendering to irrationality however. He has to do his best under the circumstances, and the best he can do is to refer to the historical distribution of prices.

I will assume that the historical distribution is a reasonably stable distribution with finite variance. This is the blandest possible staring point and it suffices for the purposes of this analysis. The distribution that is relevant to the market maker is the predictive distribution, the distribution of price change starting from the current last price. While deviations from the fixed equilibrium price are transitory, the rate of return is slow and uncertain, judged from the perspective of a market maker, so the mean of the distribution is close to the last price. The stochastic properties of this distribution are derived as some sort of convolution of the uninformative orders, so this amounts to assuming that they follow some stationary and reasonably well behaved distribution. In any case, the market maker recognizes that as long as he is exposed to the market, he is running very high risk from further bolts of lightning. He must bid low enough—in terms of a number of standard deviations below the historical mean—and offer high enough to be confident of getting to safety in a short time. This process is potentially explosive because one of these quotes is going to wind up as the next observation in the historical distribution. It is impossible, for instance, for every market maker to fix his bid at minus three standard deviations and his ask at plus three. That would result in a distribution that had all its weight beyond the three standard deviation mark! In order for the distribution to be stable, market makers have to be more aggressive, or less paranoid, than that. In any case, it is clear that a market with only market makers and uneconomic agents would be perfectly inefficient. That is not perhaps a very interesting example however, because in any real market there are also speculators present.

Adding speculators to the cast actually does not improve the efficiency of this market at all, although it may lessen the cost of market making. The market is inefficient because some agents continue to trade—the non-economic agents—even though there is no informational reason to do so. The question that we need to address here is whether speculators might at least serve to reduce the variance of prices. The answer is no.

Speculators do not reduce price variance because, quite simply, they are irrational traders.

It is a given in our model market that speculators

have no actual information that the other agents are lacking. Actually, the market makers, who at least get to see the order flow, have all the meager information that is present in the market. It is for that reason that they are able to earn a living on the bid—ask spread. The speculators have a general sort of information, which is that over time the price tends to return to the unchanging equilibrium. When it is below this point, they may be inclined to buy. To the extent that they bid more aggressively than the market makers do, they take on some of the market making risk. It is nearly as likely in practice that speculators will do the opposite, which is to sell when the price appears to be trending down and buy when it appears to be trending up. It is in any case not necessary to attempt here to characterize speculative trading strategies. The point is that they are guessing.

Periodically, they will as a group have an accumulated profit in their position, and they will start to close out positions for that reason. Assume for the sake of argument that the speculators are long. The price will start to fall accordingly, and any laggards will be motivated to sell also. At other times they, speculators, will have accumulated losses, and they will start to hit stops. Both events are also entirely unpredictable and generate waves of orders from other speculators. From the perspective of the market makers, orders from this source are no different in any way from orders from non-economic agents. The net effect is to increase the variance of net supply and demand, and therefore to increase the variance of the price.

Not only do speculators introduce an essentially random component of orders, but their orders are highly bunched. When stops are hit the price starts to move for no discernable reason, and other speculators are forced to their stops sequentially. As a result orders come in surges of buying or selling.

In the very long run, speculators can not survive in an inefficient market because they have no informational advantage, and they have to pay out the bid—ask spread that keeps market makers going. It is fair to ask, indeed, why they will have started in the first place. The reason is accidental. In any market, because of runs of net buying or selling, the price will exhibit trend. This is in a sense more pronounced in an efficient market, both because the equilibrium price can have a trend component and because traders and investors do not fully appreciate the implications of a trend when it first appears. It is not immediately evident in which markets the equilibrium price is in fact constant. Accidental runs, or more often runs generated as a matter of policy by non-economic agents, will in any case give the appearance of trend even in the absence of a trend in fundamentals. At that point, speculators who have been riding the trend will have embedded profits. Other speculators will want to share in the bonanza and will enter to take positions on the same side. This of course reinforces the trend, and sets in motion a transient wave that is fundamentally similar to a Ponzi scheme. As with any Ponzi scheme, the latecomers are ultimately fleeced, and only the nimble come out with a profit.

To summarize, a market that consists of three sorts of agents—market makers, speculators, and non-economic players—will support in equilibrium a positive variance of price even in the absence of any information flow. The price path will ultimately be highly mean reverting. Price action is all transitory. The random and inexplicable nature of price shocks will make it highly undesirable for economic agents to hold inventory of any positions. Market makers will widen their bid—ask spreads so as to be able to exit positions at a profit in a short time. Speculators too will adapt to the price shocks by progressively shortening their holding period: taking profits more aggressively and tightening their stops. Only non-economic agents can hold inventory, because they are immune to cost.

Other Agents

There are admittedly not many purely non-economic agents in the world. Even though several of them are immense, they represent in total only a small portion of all orders that enter any actual market. There are however far more agents of what we might term ambiguous motives. Take for instance the case of a large industrial corporation that is issuing new bonds. They are by any measure an economic agent, but their costs and benefits are only marginally dependent on the daily level of interest rates. They are issuing because they want or need the proceeds of the underwriting. They are going to get the money. They would prefer a lower coupon to a higher one, but that is almost sure to be a relative minor consideration. If their balance sheet demands it, they will issue when yields are high. They are fully economic agents, but their rationale is very different from, and is essentially independent of, the reasoning of an investor or speculator in bonds.

There is another class of agents who are also fully economic, but whose rationale also differs from the accepted model of the investor or trader. These are large agents who have to recognize the price impact of their actions, and who, on the other hand, have some capacity to manipulate markets in their favor. The degree of concentration of trading in many markets is not widely appreciated. It is estimated that one mutual fund complex, Fidelity, is so large that it is either the buyer or seller in one quarter of all equity transactions. One quarter of the time one of us goes to buy or sell shares, we are buying them from or selling them to Fidelity. This is of course the extreme example. There could hardly be two institutions of that magnitude, but the concentration of trading extends beyond that. In the stock market, the widespread use of passive index funds has taken a large portion of all existing shares out of the daily trading float. Shares that attract a wide retail following—the technology stocks for instance—still have a large trading float held by investors, but the old blue chip names are not widely held in tradable accounts. A very large portion of the tradable float of those names—especially the Dow Industrial names—is in the hands of a small number of large institutions, and the market for those shares is very different from the usual model presented in the Finance literature.

What these agents have in common is that their decisions are not solely driven by information of the type envisioned in the theory of financial markets. They make decisions, and have their impact on price, to some degree independently of any information about underlying value, and so their decisions hit the market much like decisions made by non-economic agents.

To sum up this account, I would like to present some empirical evidence on daily market patterns.

Evidence of Transitory Shocks in Price

There are now many statistical tests designed to detect a transitory component of a time series of data. I will use one which is simple and intuitive. Any time series—like a stock or index price series—which exhibits only permanent shocks has the property that the variance of the price grows linearly with the length of the holding period. That is to say, if we observe the price each day and compute the variance of one-day prices changes, we will get an estimate of the one-day price variance. If we instead observe the price only at two-day intervals and compute the variance of two-day price changes, we should get two times that number. In general, the variance over periods of N days should be N times the one day variance. If the price series contains a transitory component which persists for several days, the computed variance over shorter intervals of time will be larger because shocks that contribute to the variance over short intervals have washed out over long ones. To the extent that there is a transitory component of price, when we calculate price variance over longer intervals, therefore, the estimate should decrease as the holding period grows. We have to scale our estimate however so that regardless of the actual holding period, what we are measuring is in units of an equivalent one day variance.

I applied this text to six very liquid markets: the S&P and Nasdaq stock indices, the Bond contract, Gold, the Federal Reserve's index of the world value of the dollar, and the Yen/dollar exchange rate. The Fed index is of course not traded as such, but the component currencies are. The results of this test are summarized in the accompanying chart.

In every case, the measured daily variance is smaller

Daily Equivalent Standard Deviation

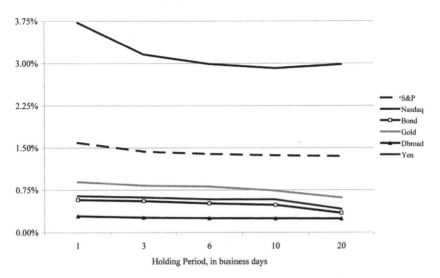

Source: Logistic Research & Trading Co.

over longer holding periods. The data used in these calculations was for the latest three hundred trading days, but the result is not sensitive to the historical period chosen. Comparable statistics calculated using the period since December 1st, 1995 exhibit exactly the same characteristic.

For all series except the Fed index of the value of the dollar, actual daily price variance is larger than the average daily price variance calculated from longer holding periods, and in fact the per day variance decreases steadily as the holding period is lengthened.

No one would leap from these findings to the conclusion that any of these markets is perfectly inefficient, but it is equally hard to ignore the presence of transitory price shocks that are inconsistent with market efficiency.

Conclusion

The proposition that transitory volatility is symptomatic of inefficiency is not novel. It is in fact simply the converse of the well known random walk characterization of the efficient market. What has not been adequately appreciated up to the present time is that, undesirable as it may be, inefficiency is also an equilibrium phenomenon, and a persistent transitory component of volatility is not at all unlikely. The reason for this, to summarize the argument I have made above, is that inefficiencies punish agents who hold inventory of open positions. The resulting attempt to earn and to take profits quickly has two effects: it exacerbates the volatility of price and it undermines the forward-looking incentives of agents, which promote efficiency.

Historically, the stock market has been the most efficient market in America, because the market participants are most clearly motivated by trading and investing profits. The market for government securities—the Treasury yield curve—has been less efficient because of the impact of decisions by our Treasury and Federal Reserve, and also companion moves by foreign Treasuries and central banks.[4] The market for foreign exchange is the least efficient because it is the one that is most consistently and aggressively managed by policy decisions of governments.

Governments and their various agencies are not very sympathetic to the havoc that they wreak in capital markets. It is their position that the markets exist to serve the needs of the nation, which is principally to take up bonds when the government wants to borrow. Policy makers in the government assume that the markets are up to the task, because there is no appetizing alternative than to assume that. Whether it is always true however remains to be seen.

Notes

1. In the depression of 1980–82, profits of the Fed exceeded the combined profits of all depository institutions.
2. A Stop is a standing order to close out an open position at a pre-set price. For instance, a trader who shorted a stock at $50 might enter a buy-stop at a higher price, say $60, to limit his loss if the shares start to go against him.
3. That is, a standing order to close out an open position at a more favorable price. The trader who shorted stock at $50 might enter a limit order to buy at $40, in order to bank his $10 gain.
4. The failure of the Treasury bond market to validate the Expectations Hypothesis is also evidence of inefficiency, and that evidence is independent of my volatility evidence.

19

Market Inefficiency As an Absorbing State

"Nothing is more irrational than a rational policy in an irrational world."

—John Manard Keynes

In the previous chapter I argued that under plausible conditions a market can continue to function in the complete absence of information flow at all. In this essay I will pursue that topic further. This point that I will make is that inefficiency is an absorbing state. Market inefficiencies devalue information. If at a point in time information trades[1] contribute a sufficiently small portion of the total variance of price, information will become irrelevant and in time the market will iterate toward the perfectly inefficient equilibrium without regard to actual information.

The market I will examine is populated by the three kinds of participants that I introduced in the earlier essay: market makers, speculators, and non-economic agents. A market maker is a profit-seeking agent that takes long and short positions in the items being traded, and that makes in profits primarily from the bid—ask spread. A speculator is also a profit-seeking agent, but it pays the bid—ask spread. Its profits come from anticipat-

253

ing price changes. Non-economic agents are indifferent to trading profits and losses, and their trading activity is initiated by entirely different stimuli than the prospect of gain. The essential difference between market makers and speculators is that speculators initiate orders while market makers respond to orders.

Information Trading

Information trades are ones that are motivated by some insight into the expected price change of the underlying instrument. I will assume for the sake of argument that speculators as a group have insight. Each individual speculator believes, when he enters a position, that he possesses valuable insight, but that may not in fact be correct. In any case, insight is only partial, and what each speculator believes he knows is a predictive distribution of the future price at a predetermined horizon. He acknowledges from the start that his information only narrows the range of plausible outcomes, and that it generally has little or nothing to say about how long he will have to wait for his ideas to be validated. The length of the horizon is part of the information set, and differs across speculators. Thus, one speculator might think that he has an insight into a report that will be issued the next morning, while another is convinced that he has insight into the capabilities of corporate management that will be revealed in consistently superior profits for a long time to come.

In an efficient market this sort of unique insight is rewarded. Efficiency actually requires the party that possesses unique insight be rewarded immediately and in full. When the possessor of unique insight comes to the market to enter a position based on his ideas, the efficient market theory asserts that whatever knowledge he brings is immediately revealed to everyone. The strict demands of the efficient market theory preclude anyone else earning trading profits by trading on information that has already been revealed to the market. This is not to say that the market equilibrium shift instantly to the price that the informed speculator anticipated. We can illustrate this point by using a single issue of stock as an example. Let the stock be priced at $20, and supposed an informed speculator has become convinced that the shares are worth $40. When he buys some shares, the price will move higher, but not necessarily all the way to $40. The reason is that he is informed but he is not omniscient. It is very possible that there is a rival speculator in the market who has reason to think that while the shares are perhaps cheap at $20, they would be wildly overvalued at $40. The bull, having taken his long position when the shares were at $20, will note with some chagrin that the rally seems to stall out well shot of his $40 target, but he would not be surprised. Experience would have taught him that very rarely do positions work out exactly as he had anticipated.

The foregoing example makes clear that an efficient market is a realistic possibility. At one time there was simplistic characterization of efficiency which seemed to imply that everyone already knows everything and therefore has no reason at all to ever buy or sell anything. The absurdity of this characterization—the absurdity of assuming that a market was perpetually in a state that would make the market itself irrelevant—was regularly turned back on the Efficient Markets Hypothesis and offered as proof that efficiency is a logical impossibility. Markets can however be efficient, and this well-known characterization is nothing more than a canard. Efficiency only requires that all speculative profits go to those who bring new information to the market, and that no one can profit by simply exploiting the market process itself.

The role of market makers has to be looked at in this light. They in fact do profit by exploiting the market process itself. That is to say, they earn a fee for simply effecting trading without necessarily having any unique insight of their own. Now, in practice, market makers do speculate in the shares in which they make markets, so all actual market makers also seek to exploit information, but in theory it is not necessarily for them to do so. If market makers earn excessive profits by maintaining excessively wide bid—ask spreads, or if their actions introduce transient bubbles in prices that take some time to be corrected, then the market is not very efficient. While it is logically possible that a market would be almost perfectly efficient—that transitory price bubbles be small and disappear rapidly—that is by no means certain. We want to investigate in this essay what happens when inefficiencies begin to account for a large share of the price variance.

Partially Efficient Markets

It has always been understood that actual markets are more or less efficient. The standard of perfect efficiency was considered to be a benchmark against which to judge the performance of markets. Initial tests of market efficiency generally supported the view that the stock market is rather highly efficient, but the statistical model used for those tests were later shown to be rather weak.

Over the last two decades or more a vast body of empirical research has overthrown the initial conclusion. At the present time it would be fair to conclude that the stock market appears to be rather efficient, but by no means perfectly efficient. Similar tests applied to other markets have come to rather different conclusions, in the sense that they consistently appear to be far much less efficient. The market for foreign exchange in particular has also been studied extensively, with the conclusion being that foreign exchange markets are not very efficient at all. This body of empirical research has been focused on characterizing the degree of efficiency on average—of estimating the correlation between unobservable "fair value" and actual market prices—and the results are very valuable for that purpose. We will take it as given that actual markets exist in some intermediary state, between perfect efficiency and perfect inefficiency. Our attention focuses elsewhere. Specifically, we ask

Is there a dynamic in a partially efficient market that drives it either toward greater efficiency or toward greater inefficiency?

The answer we propose is that

Inefficiency rewards inefficiency and punishes efficiency, and that consequently markets tend, other things being equal, to become less efficient over time.

Speculative Behavior and Efficiency

As mentioned above, we group market players conceptually into three groups: market makers, speculators, and non-economic agents. We need not dwell on the role of non-economic agents because their actions are not motivated by what is going on in the underlying fair values of the things that are traded in the market. The truly non-economic agents, like central banks, are motivated by policy concerns that are very often adopted precisely because they defy economic logic. After all, central banks and industry regulators would hardly be needed simply to ratify what the economic agents bring about by their trading decisions. The role of government authority in this context is precisely its capacity to defy the tide, and hopefully to reverse it.

In the previous essay on perfectly inefficient markets, market makers played a central role. That is because a perfectly inefficient market is in essence one in which information has become useless and observed price behavior is simply the byproduct of a very wide bid—ask spread. In that essay I assumed, for purposes of discussion, that the market in question is one in which there is in fact no information at all. That assumption reduced that analytical problem to one of showing that price variance would not disappear. The essential dynamic is that irrational price volatility is pure risk—risk for which there is no corresponding return—and that the defensive response of market makers would actually exacerbate inefficiency.

It is not necessary however to assume that there is in fact no information flow. What is essential is that trading decisions—the decisions made by market makers, speculators, and non-economic agents alike—are not responsive to available information. A market will be perfectly inefficient if the players simply ignore the kinds of information that would, in better circumstances, result in efficient pricing.

More generally, a market will be rather inefficient if the players choose rationally to ignore information because it has become too risky to use it.

Since it is speculators—a category that includes the more familiar category of "investors"—who initiate information trades, this analysis must be directed at their incentives and their behavior. If they worsen inefficiency, market makers will react accordingly by widening their bid—spread. What we need to understand is how inefficiencies—random, transitory price shocks—devalue information.

Information and Information Trades

Information is knowledge about the course of future events. We can usefully adopt the statistical model in which information, as it is modeled in statistics, is knowledge about the distribution of some future outcome. The quantity of information is, in effect, the degree to which the informed distribution is more precise, narrower, and the uninformed one. A familiar example, pitching pennies, illustrates this idea. Whenever you guess correctly the next throw, you keep the penny. When you guess wrong, you lose one of your own pennies. A priori, heads and tails are equally likely. Suppose however that the pennies are actually weighted to land heads 75% of the time. Information consists of knowing this actual probability of a head. It is limited information, in the sense that the next actual outcome is still unpredictable, but over time one can be fairly sure to make money by always betting on heads.[2]

Another example of information brings the concept closer to a financial perspective. The stock market encompasses thousands of individual corporations. We naturally think of the shares of a single company in terms of two factors: the expected price change of the shares over some period of time and the expected variance of actual outcomes around the expectation. The actual results for any given company are uncertain, and the variance quantifies just how uncertain they are. The company is modeled statistically as the mean and variance of its specific return distribution.[3] When we look at all the companies together, another source of uncertainty or variation arises: co-variation between different companies. When we have gained specific insight about a particular firm, it is the variance of the firm-specific distribution that applies. When we merely survey the whole field of firms without having any information that is specific to one of them, then all of them appear to be the same. The variance of outcomes for any particular firm in that case is the sum of the specific variance of a typical firm and the variance across firms. To gain information about a single firm is, then, to differentiate it from the rest and to specialize the predictive distribution of its outcomes.

Fundamental research about a business or an industry fits neatly into this pattern. When we start to analyze the firms in a given industry, all of them appear to be the same. That is to say, while we know the firms differ, we have no specific information about these firms that would identify the more successful from the less successful. There is no alternative but to treat them as equals until we get a clearer picture of their difference. If we were to try to project the outcome of a given firm we would have to allow that it might be the most productive firm in the industry and that moreover it might be especially favored. On the other hand, it might be consistently the worst laggard, and suffer bad luck over the horizon to which we are making projections. There is an unpredictable element that no amount of research will anticipate, but we can narrow the range of projected outcomes by discerning where the firm ranks on the spectrum form most productive to least productive in the industry.

Information is by its nature incomplete. It never happens that even the most informed speculator would know the future with perfect certainty. Some variance of outcomes remains, and it has two implications. First, of course, is that the speculative position will actually turn out to be more or less profitable than expected. Second, and for our purposes more importantly, the speculator can't know in advance how reliable his insight is. If the results are disappointing, there is no way to know whether the disappointment was the result of bad luck or bad information. He has his sources of fundamental research, as I have outlined it, but he also confronts a constant flow of feedback from the market itself. He knows that his fundamental research is incomplete, and may be highly incomplete. He knows furthermore that he has no objective basis to judge how complete or incomplete it is. He must ultimately guess how valuable is his initial body of information. He must also guard himself against the worst cases. His fortunes are suspended between two competing forces: the value of the insight that he brings to the market on the one side, and the inexorable logic of gambler's ruin on the other.

The law of gambler's ruin is a mathematical law

which states that almost surely anyone who continues to wager his limited capital will eventually lose it all. However much capital any one speculator has, it is very small compared with the combined capital of the rest of the world, and so it is appropriate to assume that he is playing against an opponent that has unlimited capital. If the speculator has no special insight at all—if he is merely guessing—then it is certain that he will eventually lose all his capital. If he has some real insight, he will at least survive longer, and if his edge is greater than some threshold he can expect to survive indefinitely. His edge has to be quite large, as measured in units of expected profit per play of the game, for that to happen. The typical speculator is understandably, and perhaps justifiably, convinced that he has some valuable knowledge, and that he has therefore a positive expected profit per trade, but if he is realistic, he accepts that he is unlikely to defy the law of gambler's ruin indefinitely. It is advisable for him to try to supplement his trading offensive—which utilizes his knowledge—with a solid risk-management defensive. The defensive—various forms of stop-loss tactics—must necessarily be independent of his offense. He must be willing to take defensive measures even against the counsel of his trading knowledge because the very purpose of the defensive is to prevent an over-commitment to his beliefs and insight. If he places stop points that seem to be a good place to get out based on his knowledge, then he is not reducing his risk, he is doubling it.

These observations apply even in a perfectly efficient market. Even in such a market, any given speculator will win if he possesses a great deal of information or he will at least survive for some period of time before his capital is gone. If inefficiencies are present, then the odds shift radically against even the most insightful speculator.

Two forces are at work to diminish the value of information, and or even to make it a liability. The first is that the speculator can not be certain of the accuracy or reliability of his information and the conclusions he has drawn from it. When price movement is influenced by a transitory price run, he has no way of knowing if this is merely a transient event, or if it is evidence that his assumptions are wrong. Suppose, for definiteness, that the speculator is long, and that the price is rising much faster than he had anticipated. He knows that either he underestimated how good the news would be—that is to say, actual developments have exceeded the prior expected value—or he is witnessing a transient price bubble. Experience has taught him however that it is wise to take a profit because profits often prove to be fleeting. On the other side, if the price has fallen he again cannot know if he is witnessing a permanent or transitory event. In both cases, the price path frequently, or even generally, reflects outcomes that were not contemplated by his initial information. He is forced rationally to question his prior ideas.

At the same time that the speculator is depreciating the accuracy of his information, the variance of outcomes is forcing him to tighten his risk management, to reinforce stop-losses and to tighten profit-taking. This is prudent and necessary because of the logic of gambler's ruin, and it operates even if the speculator refuses to let his commitment to his initial research weaken. It happens because the ratio of expected price variance to total variance is lower. To summarize, transitory—but often prolonged—price bubbles cause the speculator to lose confidence in his information while at the same time causing him to apply risk management methods more aggressively. His expected return from entering a position is no longer the expected value given that what he knows is true and accurate, because of the cost of risk management and because of the cost of giving up on positions that are in fact justified by all available information. But though his expected value is lower, the variance of outcomes is greater. Depending on the magnitude of the transitory surges in relation to the variance of the permanent component of price, the speculator reaches a point where even though his ideas are sound, the expected value of his trades is negative. He simply cannot afford to utilize his knowledge.

This logic operates at the level of the individual, but when we aggregate across the whole market of speculators, a third ingredient becomes apparent, which further reduces the value of information. Since speculators are as a whole informed traders, the position taken by the average speculator is correlated with the direction of incoming information. In other words, most speculators will be positioned on the side of the market that gives the positive expected profit in light of what is known. That implies however that most speculators will at any given time and in any given market be on the same side of the trade, either long or short. Events that defy the prior knowledge and that force defensive actions therefore strike most traders at the same time! There is an understandable exodus from positions that have lost support. This greatly enlarges the transient component of price. Many speculators, clinging to some commitment to their prior convictions, will refuse to panic. They will hold out in the belief that they are witnessing a temporary panic, and for the most part they will be right. They can expect to be right often, but they also know that they cannot afford to be wrong very often at all.

Depending on the contribution of transitory bubbles to the total variance of price, information can become a liability. Speculators attempting to survive in such a market environment will be well advised—assumed that they do not wish to simply find another career—to find technical trading methods that are intended to exploit the inefficiencies of the market. At that point, the market ceases to respond to information at all, because no one is willing to take a position based on it. In that situation the market is effectively perfectly inefficient, because while underlying market equilibrium is not constant, and there is revealing information available, it does not pay anyone to try to exploit that information. This analysis suggests the following hypothesis, which I think merits definitive modeling work:

There is a critical threshold for the variance of the transitory component of price variance above which the market becomes effectively perfectly inefficient. The threshold is a function of the variance of the informational component of value and of the expected drift rate of price. The lower the drift rate—the lower the maximum expected return from information trading—the lower is the threshold.

This conjecture raises in a very natural way a further question, which is whether any inefficiency at all triggers a descent to this threshold. It would obviously be regrettable in the extreme if that is true, and I do not think that it is. More likely it is that there is something like a second threshold with the property that any market which initially is that efficient or more is stable. While my analysis thus far has seemed to diminish the value of information, that is not true. Information is very valuable as long as it is recognized by the market as a whole in a reasonably prompt manner. Uncertainty about how rapidly a market will adjust to even the most insightful information is as important as the risk if intervening transitory runs in devaluating information. These risks are, as it were, partners in crime. There is a further consideration that tends, however, to enhance the value of information. In any market in which it is possible to diversify specific risk, a speculator can remain fully, or almost fully, invested while taking quite small positions in individual trading instruments. The American stock market has historically been a model of the potential for diversification.

Diversification is real risk reduction, but it requires the speculator to have valuable information about many different specific risks, because he is exposed to many specific risks. A large institution with very deep capital—a mutual fund complex for instance—could probably afford to obtain and process such a broad agenda of information, and to build a highly diversified portfolio as a result. In recent times however even this recourse has been less effective because financial assets of all kinds have become much more highly correlated than they were historically. Not only are individual share issues more correlated with each other, they are more correlated with foreign shares, with domestic interest rates, and with foreign exchange. The commodization of equities, which is itself a byproduct of the greatly increased appetite for speculative trading, has diminished the potential defensive value of diversification, I will not attempt to pursue this point further at this time, but will conclude with the observation that a speculator who has valuable information about many alternative instruments that are not too highly correlated with each other can very probably succeed even in the presence of significant inefficiencies. It goes without saying that no speculator can succeed in a perfectly inefficient market, regardless of what trading tactics he uses.

In the foregoing analysis I have equated markets that are in some respects very different. That is to say, I treated a market that is unresponsive to information as being the same as one in which there is simply no information at all. That needs some explanation. If the prospects of the instruments that are traded in the market changes over time, and if accordingly equilibrium price evolves over time, the market cannot perpetually defy the implications of information. If, to take a concrete example, the instrument is shares of a corporation that is rather successful and earns a high rate of return on its investments, then in the very long run the shares must rise. It does not follow however that the market is even slightly efficient in practice. If the shares react to good news in a discontinuous way—if they fail to respond for a long time and then adjust suddenly and explosively—the value of information about the operations of the firm will be almost without value. This example illustrates the edge that an informed and highly diversified speculator can have. He can simply position a small block of the shares and wait for the inevitable correction. As long as he is both right about the true underlying value of the shares and refuses to surrender to the market's rejection of his beliefs, he will eventually be paid for what he knows. If his position is small enough, he can presumably wait almost indefinitely for the truth to come out. The fact remains however that in general explosive or discontinuous corrections, even if they are corrections toward equilibrium values, diminish the value of information.

The argument that I have advanced here hinges on the prospect for speculators, but the analysis is not complete until we consider the situation of the other kinds of market participants: market makers, non-economic agents, and a third category that I will designate "buy and hold" players.

Market Makers

It is not necessary to add anything here to the analysis of market makers, above and beyond the analysis found in my previous essay, "The Perfectly Inefficient Market." Market inefficiencies are a byproduct of their defensive tendency to widen the bid—ask spread. At any given time, market makers will quote what seem to be narrow spreads, but quoted bid—ask spreads are irrelevant for two reasons. First, they are good only for small orders, but transitory price bubbles are the result of persistent order imbalance representing large total volume of transactions. Quoted spreads are irrelevant also because they are biased. At any given point in time, the majority of orders that a market maker receives are on one side or the other. Suppose he is experiencing a run of sell orders as speculators dump positions. If asked, the market maker will quote bid and ask, but they don't mean the same thing. The bid he quotes is real; he is probably going to have to buy at the price. But the ask is hypothetical. There is a little interest on the part of the public in buying and so he is unlikely to be taken out no matter what ask he quotes. A few contrarians can exploit this imbalance to accumulate small positions at aggressive ask prices, and if the market stabilizes or recovers they will profit, but the profits that they earn—extracted from the market maker—are small compared with what the market maker earns from lowering his bid.

Non-economic Agents

The situation of the non-economic agents is unchanged in many ways. They are able to continue to pursue their goals without regard to what is happening in the market. That is why they are a source of transitory price shocks. Some of the largest non-economic agents however are susceptible to a feedback of the following sort.

The very largest of the non-economic agents are the world's central banks. They pursue an agenda based on the needs and interests of the nation, or perhaps those of the governing party, that they serve. Those interests are themselves impacted by many markets, and for this reason the bankers will assume some responsibility for the success of the markets. The natural and almost inevitable result is that they will try to use their vast capital to steer the wayward market back to proper behavior. In Japan, for instance, the Treasury simply buys shares of stock in a futile attempt to increase their value. The problem with these actions is that they do not make the market More efficient—they do not make it more responsive to important information—they must make it Less efficient. Who indeed would waste time to learn anything about any of the instruments if the prices are simply going to be fixed by the central bank anyway? The presence of non-economic agents is a very difficult burden for a market to cope with, but it is not ordinarily impossible to do it. If, however, those agents take it upon themselves to aggressively exploit their impact on market performance there is really little hope of restoring any degree of efficiency.

Buy and Hold Investors

Do buy and hold investors make a market more efficient? That can hardly be the case, because they are actually absent from the market. The premise of buy and hold is that the world would be a better place if there were no market at all. Specifically, buy and hold has the effect of converting publicly traded instruments into private placements. We need not dwell here on a lengthy analysis of whether this approach works or not, though the rolls of corporate bankruptcy filings cannot be ignored on that point. Since buy and hold investors do not trade, they actually have no impact on a market. For practical purposes, buy-and-hold is a policy for equity investors. Their importance in the context of this essay arises from how many of them there are and how much of the whole pool of outstanding shares they command. Individual investors are very patient investors, to the extent that the shares they own need to be subtracted from the tradable float of the stock market. What remains is a much smaller market, populated by agents with much shorter decision horizons than is generally appreciated.

Conclusion

The argument which I have advanced in this essay does not depend on any novel hypotheses or on any obscure mathematics. It rests two familiar consequences of randomness. One consequence is that speculators, like everyone else, learn from experience. When what we know is only a probability distribution of outcomes, it is impossible to be certain in advance of what we know. Since we are not certain about what is going to happen, we must constantly grope along, seeking confirming and discomfirming evidence. When that evidence arises, we adapt our expectations to it. Since transitory bubbles and shocks are indistinguishable from discomfirming evidence, they necessarily, and indeed rationally, shake our confidence in what we initially thought we knew. These are the terms under which we all operate in life and speculators are not exempt from the implications.

The other consequence is summed in the rule called Gambler's Ruin. Anyone who continues to gamble with limited capital against a market that has effectively unlimited capital is very likely to lose everything. A rather large expected profit on each play of the game is needed to make repeated gambling a viable activity. Faced with this fact, a rational speculator will attempt to supplement his stock of information, his trading asset, with risk management tools intended to conserve capital.

Under these circumstances, in the face of market inefficiencies even genuine information can easily become a liability rather than an asset. Successful speculators will not rely on information, but will rely on technical trading rules that are intended to exploit the inefficiencies in a purely mechanical way. At that point, market clearing prices cease to respond to information because, quite simply, actual trading decisions do not reflect available information.

Notes

1. Information trades are transactions motivated by ideas and knowledge about matters external to the market itself. Technical trading—trades motivated by the trading record of the market—is not a kind of information trading. Similarly, noise trading—trades motivated by considerations specific to the trader—are not information trades.
2. It is not absolutely certain that one would make money, because de-

pending on how much capital one has initially to gamble with it is possible to lose the entire stake before the law of averages comes to the rescue.

3. There is a third set of parameters, which consists of the correlations between the results for the particular firm and external, conditioning events. Among the correlations is the set of correlations between the particular firm and all other firms. These correlations play a central role in how one gains information about the firm, but it is not central to the point we are making.